Cambridge Elements ≡

Elements in Publishing and Book Culture
edited by
Samantha Rayner
University College London
Leah Tether
University of Bristol

ENTREPRENEURIAL IDENTITY IN US BOOK PUBLISHING IN THE TWENTY-FIRST CENTURY

Rachel Noorda
Portland State University

CAMBRIDGE
UNIVERSITY PRESS

CAMBRIDGE
UNIVERSITY PRESS

University Printing House, Cambridge CB2 8BS, United Kingdom

One Liberty Plaza, 20th Floor, New York, NY 10006, USA

477 Williamstown Road, Port Melbourne, VIC 3207, Australia

314–321, 3rd Floor, Plot 3, Splendor Forum, Jasola District Centre,
New Delhi – 110025, India

103 Penang Road, #05–06/07, Visioncrest Commercial, Singapore 238467

Cambridge University Press is part of the University of Cambridge.

It furthers the University's mission by disseminating knowledge in the pursuit of
education, learning, and research at the highest international levels of excellence.

www.cambridge.org
Information on this title: www.cambridge.org/9781108819510
DOI: 10.1017/9781108875974

First published 2021

A catalogue record for this publication is available from the British Library.

ISBN 978-1-108-81951-0 Paperback
ISSN 2514-8524 (online)
ISSN 2514-8516 (print)

Entrepreneurial Identity in US Book Publishing in the Twenty-First Century

Elements in Publishing and Book Culture

DOI: 10.1017/9781108875974

First published online: September 2021

Rachel Noorda

Portland State University

Author for correspondence: Rachel Noorda, rnoorda@pdx.edu

ABSTRACT: Entrepreneurship underpins many roles within the publishing industry, from freelancing to bookselling. Entrepreneurs are shaped by the contexts in which their entrepreneurship is situated (social, political, economic, and national). Additionally, entrepreneurship is integral to occupational identity for book publishing entrepreneurs. This Element examines entrepreneurship through the lens of identity and narrative based on interview data with book publishing entrepreneurs in the US. Book publishing entrepreneurship narratives of independence, culture over commerce, accidental profession, place, risk, (in)stability, busyness, and freedom are examined in this Element.

KEYWORDS: entrepreneurship, freelancing, narrative, bookselling, occupational identity

ISBNs: 9781108819510 (PB), 9781108875974 (OC)
ISSNs: 2514-8524 (online), 2514-8516 (print)

Contents

Introduction

Entrepreneurship in the United States

In the graduate programme in book publishing that I lead at Portland State University, students enter the programme with a variety of aspirational endeavours: many of them want to be editors and dream of working for a large publishing house in New York City as an in-house editor with their own list of award-winning titles. There are still individuals who live this dream, but a 'traditional' path such as this in the book industry is far from traditional nowadays. Those who succeed best in the book industry exercise flexibility and agility through innovative entrepreneurship: starting their own publishing houses, freelancing, and carving out new roles and careers to fit changing industry needs and dynamics. Down (2006) has gone so far as to say that entrepreneurship is 'a contemporary economic necessity' in the twenty-first century for those establishing their careers and occupational identities.[1]

According to the US Small Business Administration, in 2020 there were 31.7 million small businesses in the United States, which represent 99 per cent of all US businesses and employ 60.6 million people – 47.1 per cent of all US employees.[2] In other words, small businesses – upheld as a pinnacle of entrepreneurship – are the foundation of the US economy. It is estimated that for the creative industries (which includes the book industry), self-employment is even higher than for the average American: for example, artists are 'highly entrepreneurial' and 3.6 times more likely to be self-employed than the general US workforce.[3] Thus, entrepreneurship (at least in the self-employment sense) is high in the United States, and even higher within the creative industries.

---

[1] S. Down, *Narratives of Enterprise: Crafting Entrepreneurial Self-Identity in a Small Firm* (Cheltenham/Northampton, MA: Elgar Publishing, 2006), p. 114.

[2] US Small Business Administration Office of Advocacy, '2020 Small Business Profile', 2020, https://cdn.advocacy.sba.gov/wp-content/uploads/2020/06/04144224/2020-Small-Business-Economic-Profile-US.pdf

[3] National Assembly of State Arts Agencies, 'Facts and Figures on the Creative Economy', 2020, https://nasaa-arts.org/nasaa_research/facts-figures-on-the-creative-economy/

Juxtaposed with this entrepreneurial environment is the current disruption of traditional employment, most recently because of the COVID-19 pandemic. Florida and Seman[4] estimate that there were 252,820 job losses in the publishing industry from April to July 2020, representing 9.1 per cent of jobs in the industry. In terms of occupations within or adjacent to the book industry, Florida and Seman estimate that 176,416 jobs for writers/authors, 46,813 jobs for editors, 76,838 jobs for graphic designers, and 26,339 jobs for other designers were lost between April and July 2020 due to the pandemic. The loss of traditional book industry jobs drives workers towards other options, including entrepreneurship through self-employment in the industry. The book industry is still thriving – with strong book sales during the pandemic, up 8.2 per cent in 2020[5] – but what occupations look like in the book industry continues to shift towards entrepreneurship and away from 'traditional' career paths.

Down (2006) argues that the individualization and privatization of Western society in the twentieth and twenty-first centuries have contributed to a general rise in entrepreneurship in the Western world:

> Western society is more individualised and privatised; individuals choose or must accept more risk and responsibility in their lives. Even as consumers we are targeted individually. Work has become more transient and enterprising in orientation. We are expected to be more flexible, self-reliant and entrepreneurial at work. Our organizations are changing and becoming less interested in looking after us.[6]

Thus, the COVID-19 pandemic is only the most recent exacerbation of an already growing, entrepreneurially oriented system of employment in

---

[4] R. Florida and M. Seman, 'Lost Art: Measuring COVID-19's Devastating Impact on America's Creative Economy' (2020), www.brookings.edu/wp-content/uploads/2020/08/20200810_Brookingsmetro_Covid19-and-creative-economy_Final.pdf.

[5] J. Milliot, 'Print Book Sales Rose 8.2% in 2020', *Publishers Weekly* (7 January 2021).

[6] Down, *Narratives of Enterprise*, p. 5.

the United States in the twenty-first century. Entrepreneurship is important to consider in the US book publishing industry for several reasons: book publishing is rarely the focus of academic research into entrepreneurship, the rapid rate of change in the book industry necessitates entrepreneurship more so than in other industries, and the United States fosters a particularly strong entrepreneurial national narrative to foreground self-employment behaviour within its borders. This is the best place to begin, with one of the key narratives that contextualises and encourages entrepreneurship within United States culture: the American Dream.

Entrepreneurial Narratives in the United States: The American Dream

The American Dream is a pervasive national narrative, one that shapes national identity but also other identities – occupational identity and class identity among them. The national narrative of the American Dream centres entrepreneurship at its core. This narrative shapes the perception of entrepreneurs, acceptability of entrepreneurship, and motivations for entrepreneurship. In the cultural history of the American Dream, Samuel asserts that the entrepreneurial spirit is embedded in the American Dream, along with other 'familiar tropes of the American idea and experience', including that 'tomorrow will be better than today', and the emphasis on wealth, success, hope, and change in 'the belief that anything is possible'.[7] The American Dream is one of the key national narratives that has shaped American identity, culture, politics, and business practices.

Despite the promise of the American Dream to offer social mobility to anyone who works hard enough, the data tells a different story – for example, in terms of absolute economic mobility (whether or not children make more money than their parents). In a paper from the National Bureau of Economic Research, Chetty et al. compared children's household income at age thirty to that of their parents at the same age. When tracked over time, this data reveals that while 90 per cent of children born in 1940 made more money than their parents, only 50 per cent of children born in 1980 made more money than their parents. In other words, absolute economic mobility has been steadily

---

[7] L. R. Samuel, *The American Dream: A Cultural History* (Syracuse: Syracuse University Press, 2019), p. 5.

declining in the United States since the 1940s. The authors call this phenomenon 'the fading American Dream'.[8] Intergenerational economic mobility is particularly limited for BIPOC (Black, Indigenous, and People of Color) people in the United States, especially Black communities. Here is an example: In US counties 'with a majority black population, a black child born to parents in the 25th income percentile only achieves a mean income rank of 32, barely any movement up the income ladder, while white children from the same counties achieve a mean income rank of 43'.[9] Inequalities abound in the United States, regardless of how the American Dream presents the country as a place of equal opportunity.

However, the purpose of this discussion of the American Dream narrative is to consider it as simply that – a narrative. My purpose is not to prove or disprove this narrative, but to rather explore how it (and other narratives) influence entrepreneurship in the United States. Because of the centrality of the narrative of the American Dream to American national identity and American life, entrepreneurship – particularly as manifested through small business – is universally embraced by politicians across the political spectrum in the US.[10] Being anti-small business or anti-entrepreneurship is simply something you do not see in US politics. This is illustrated simply and powerfully in US presidential speeches:

- In 1946, President Truman said, 'It is obvious national policy to foster the sound development of small business.'
- In 1956, President Eisenhower said, 'We shall continue to help small business concerns to obtain access to adequate financing and to competent counsel on management, production, and marketing problems.'

---

[8] R. Chetty, D. Grusky, M. Hell, N. Hendren, R. Manduca, and J. Narang, 'The Fading American Dream: Trends in Absolute Income Mobility Since 1940', *National Bureau of Economic Research Working Paper Series* (2016), https://opportunityin sights.org/paper/the-fading-american-dream/

[9] Equitable Growth, 'Race and the Lack of Intergenerational Economic Mobility in the United States', in *Vision 2020: Evidence for a Stronger Economy* (18 February 2020), www.equitablegrowth.org/race-and-the-lack-of-intergen erational-economic-mobility-in-the-united-states/

[10] Samuel, *The American Dream*.

- In 1962, President Kennedy said, 'This administration has helped keep our economy competitive by widening the access of small business.'
- In 1973, President Nixon expressed his objective to 'bolster small business.'
- In 1976, President Ford said, 'Also, I ask, for the sake of future generations, that we preserve the family farm and family-owned small business. Both strengthen America and give stability to our economy.'
- In 1980, President Carter said, 'I have often said that there is nothing small about small business in America.'
- In 1983, President Reagan said, 'Too often, entrepreneurs are forgotten heroes. We rarely hear about them. But look into the heart of America, and you'll see them.'
- In 2002, President George W. Bush said, 'Help for small business means jobs for Americans.'
- In 2009, President Obama said, 'All across America, even today on a Saturday, millions of Americans are hard at work. They're running the mom-and-pop stores and neighbourhood restaurants we know and love. They're building tiny start-ups with big ideas that could revolutionise an industry, maybe even transform our economy. They are the more than half of all Americans who work at a small business or own a small business. And they embody the spirit of possibility, the relentless work ethic, and the hope for something better that is at the heart of the American Dream.'

Baumol, Litan, and Schramm identify four types of capitalism: state-guided capitalism, oligarchic capitalism, big-firm capitalism, and entrepreneurial capitalism. These authors argue that the United States is a blend of big-firm capitalism and entrepreneurial capitalism. Some of the reasons why the United States reflects entrepreneurial capitalism is that the government places relatively few restrictions on those trying to start a business: 'Successful entrepreneurial economies embrace and generally encourage change. They do not erect barriers that prevent money and people from shifting from slow-moving or dying sectors to dynamic industries. They do not wall off their existing producers from more efficient ones in foreign countries.'[11] In this way, the United States supports entrepreneurs by remaining rather hands-off (i.e. not intentionally impeding growth or innovation).

However, in general, despite entrepreneurship's foundational ties to the American Dream narrative, and despite the words of many US presidents, in the United States support for small business falls short when compared to many other countries. Baumol, Litan, and Schramm acknowledge that it is not enough for entrepreneurial economies to not erect barriers; these economies must also support entrepreneurship: 'Because radical change is so disruptive, entrepreneurial economies can benefit from properly constructed safety nets that shield some of the victims of change from its harsh impacts (without at the same time destroying their initiative to get back on their feet).'[12] There are few safety nets for entrepreneurs in the United States, particularly in three important areas: healthcare, start-up funding, and institutional barriers.

One important shortcoming is in terms of healthcare. Unlike its northern neighbour, Canada, or many European countries (such as the UK), the United States does not provide its citizens with free, universal healthcare. Because of this, small businesses bear the burden of huge costs to pay for healthcare for themselves and their employees. Some entrepreneurs choose to go without healthcare for this reason, or rely on the healthcare benefits of a partner. Another shortcoming of small business support in the United States is government financial support for start-up funding. This is particularly true for the creative industries. While the Small Business Administration (established in 1953) offers some financial support to businesses, this is primarily in the form of training and informational materials rather than start-up funding. The nature of the book industry (and the creative industries as a whole) is such that margins are slim and cultural value is deemed important alongside economic value. These conditions do not attract wealthy venture capitalists.

---

[11] W. J. Baumol, R. E. Litan, and C. J. Schramm, *Good Capitalism, Bad Capitalism, and the Economics of Growth and Prosperity* (New Haven, CT: Yale University Press, 2007), p. 91.

[12] Ibid.

Because of the American Dream narrative, there is a perception in the United States that succeeding (usually only measured in terms of economic capital) as an entrepreneur is based solely on the merit and hard work of the entrepreneur. Such a view does not take into consideration factors of structural and institutional inequality that create barriers for certain entrepreneurs right from the start. While the government might not be intentionally erecting new barriers for entrepreneurial entry, the system itself is built upon policies and institutions that are racist, sexist, ableist, etc. Additionally, there are other ways to measure success beyond economic success, and this is especially important in the book industry.

What we have, then, is a positive perception of entrepreneurship and pride in national culture for entrepreneurship, but a stunning lack of systems and institutions to support entrepreneurs. This clash comes through in the stories of individual entrepreneurs (highlighted in this book) who are influenced by but also react against these forces in various ways.

This conflicting picture of entrepreneurship in the United States can be contrasted with national perspectives, narratives, and attitudes towards entrepreneurship in other nations. For example, in their interviews with female small business owners in the UK, Cohen and Musson found that perceptions of entrepreneurship from these entrepreneurs were not always positive. Cohen and Musson found that some of their interviewees saw the 'image of the entrepreneur as exploitative, associated in particular with the 1980s and Thatcher's Britain'.[13] Anderson et al., in their analysis of entrepreneurship in Stanton, New Zealand, note that 'New Zealand is culturally distinctive in its perceptions of entrepreneurship, which seems likely to influence how entrepreneurship and entrepreneurial identity is perceived', and is characterised by concepts such as 'a laidback lifestyle culture, emphasizing life balance rather than capital accumulation'.[14] These are broad generalizations of the entrepreneurship culture in the UK and New

---

[13] L. Cohen and G. Musson, 'Entrepreneurial Identities: Reflections from Two Case Studies', *Organization*, 7 (2007), p. 42.

[14] A. R. Anderson, L. Warren, and J. Bensemann, 'Identity, Enactment, and Entrepreneurship Engagement in a Declining Place', *Journal of Small Business Management*, 57 (2019), p. 1561.

Zealand, but they are broad and stereotypical in the same way that the American Dream is a broad stereotype of entrepreneurship culture in the USA, and they serve to illustrate the comparatively positive entrepreneurial perspective that the United States portrays.

Defining Entrepreneurship

As will be discussed further in the methodology section of this chapter, this book is built upon the data of entrepreneurial narratives (interviews) from thirty-nine entrepreneurs in the US book industry. Their perceptions of entrepreneurship were universally positive, which contrasts with the findings from scholars in other countries who encountered more negative perceptions of entrepreneurship from entrepreneurs. Even so, Cohen and Musson found that their interviewees did not necessarily identify with the term 'entrepreneur' regardless of whether they viewed the term as 'good' or 'bad': 'these women, whilst embracing the enterprise culture, felt that they did not have the right to claim "entrepreneur" as an occupational identity.'[15] Larson and Pearson similarly found that some participants used 'entrepreneur' to describe their occupational identities, but others focused on a particular profession or industry: 'Regardless of preferred occupational label, though, the narratives of occupational identity conveyed by our participants drew from discursive resources associated with the celebrated entrepreneur in Western market capitalism.'[16] Similarly, book industry entrepreneurs also often chose different terminology (outside of the term 'entrepreneur') to identify with, founded on why what they were doing in their own business work was beyond the constrained definition of entrepreneurship. This stems, in part, from the lack of a unified definition of entrepreneurship, both in academia and in the book industry. Even so, much like Larson and Pearson found, regardless of terminology, the occupational narratives were tied into a positive perception of entrepreneurial endeavours.

[15] Cohen and Musson, 'Entrepreneurial Identities', p. 42.

[16] G. S. Larson and A. R. Pearson, 'Placing Identity: Place as a Discursive Resource for Occupational Identity Work Among High-Tech Entrepreneurs', *Management Communication Quarterly*, 26 (2012), p. 250.

In their foundational publication on the field of entrepreneurship, Shane and Venkataraman define entrepreneurship as *the discovery, evaluation, and exploitation of opportunities to create goods and services.* Entrepreneurs are 'the set of individuals who discover, evaluate, and exploit' these opportunities.[17] This is the definition that I will be using in my discussion of entrepreneurship in the US book industry.

Twenty years after Shane and Venkataraman's groundbreaking paper and definition, *opportunities* are still central to the study of entrepreneurship.[18] However, other aspects of entrepreneurship and alternative definitions include *value creation*, *innovation*, and *risk* as key components. Entrepreneurs have been defined as the individuals 'responsible for the process of creating new value'[19] and who 'create and innovate to build something of recognised value around perceived opportunities'.[20] Value creation and innovation implies that entrepreneurship is exploiting, discovering, and evaluating opportunities in different or unique ways.

The concept of risk is also a key component of many definitions of entrepreneurship and, indeed, of the field and study of entrepreneurship. For example, Dollinger defines entrepreneurship as the creation of an organization intended to grow, but under particular 'conditions of risk and uncertainty'.[21] Similarly, Mokaya, Namusonge, and Sikalieh acknowledge that entrepreneurs not only seize opportunities but also undertake 'to

---

[17] S. Shane and S. Venkataraman, 'The Promise of Entrepreneurship as a Field of Research', *Academy of Management Review*, 25 (2000), p. 218.

[18] S. Alvarez and J. B. Barney, 'Has the Concept of Opportunities Been Fruitful In the Field of Entrepreneurship?', *Academy of Management Perspectives*, 34 (2020), 300–10.

[19] C. Bruyat and P. A. Julien, 'Defining the Field of Research in Entrepreneurship', *Journal of Business Venturing*, 16 (2001), 169.

[20] W. K. Bolton and J. L. Thompson, *Entrepreneurs: Talent, Tempérament, Technique* (Oxford: Butterworth Heinemann, 2000), p. 5.

[21] M. Dollinger, *Entrepreneurship* (Lombard, IL: Marsh Publications, 2008), p. 9, 28.

organize, manage and assume the risks of business and realize the rewards'.[22] In short, 'entrepreneurs assume business risks in uncertain environments'.[23]

Dempster asserts that risk is important to entrepreneurship because 'business growth and value creation depends on the relationship between losses and failures'. Therefore, risk is 'a central part of the entrepreneurial function and ultimately critical in the creation of economic value and innovation'.[24] Entrepreneurship, an environment where the possibility of great growth is offset by the possibility of severe loss, has risk at its very centre. As will become clear in this Element, risk is also a key component in the narratives that publishing entrepreneurs construct and tell about themselves.

There are five types of risk that are useful for a discussion of entrepreneurship in the creative industries: financial, competitive, reputational, natural, and operational. Financial risk is the type of risk most readily identified with entrepreneurship: namely, monetary investment that risks being lost should the business fail.[25] Competitive risk is the unpredictability of competitor actions and the resultant consequences.[26] Reputational risk is the risk of something happening that impacts a company's/entrepreneur's reputation or brand negatively. Natural risk is serendipity or luck, recognizing that 'entrepreneurial decisions alone do not determine financial

---

[22] D. Sikalieh, S. O. Mokaya, and M. Namusonge, 'The Concept of Entrepreneurship: In Pursuit of a Universally Acceptable Definition', *International Journal of Arts and Commerce*, 1 (2012), p. 30.

[23] M. Koudstaal, R. Sloof, and M. Van Praag, 'Risk, Uncertainty, and Entrepreneurship: Evidence from a Lab-in-the-Field Experiment', *Management Science*, 62 (2016), p. 2897.

[24] A. M. Dempster, 'An Operational Risk Framework for the Performing Arts and Creative Industries', *Creative Industries Journal*, 1 (2009), p. 152.

[25] M. J. Naude and N. Chiweshe, 'A Proposed Operational Risk Management Framework for Small and Medium Enterprises', *South African Journal of Economic and Management Sciences*, 20 (2017), 1–10.

[26] D. Di Gregorio, 'Re-Thinking Country Risk: Insights from Entrepreneurship Theory', *International Business Review*, 14 (2005), p. 210.

outcomes'.[27] Finally, operational risk 'deals with the internal organization and management of the operations team for development, production, supply, and distribution. Operational risk encompasses the production, warehousing, distribution, staff challenges, systems and the processes the company uses.'[28]

The creative industries are characterised by significant levels of uncertainty and risk,[29] not only in the creative industries in general, but in the publishing industry in particular. One of the primary areas of uncertainty and risk in the publishing industry is *demand uncertainty* because writers and publishers experiment and push boundaries without the evidence of need and demand that other industries would not proceed without.[30] It might be argued that the very act of publishing a book is itself an entrepreneurial activity; indeed, this very argument has been made by Sattersten, who wrote an entire volume on how every book is a start-up entrepreneurial venture.[31]

The use and understanding of the term 'entrepreneur' vary not only from person to person but also from industry to industry. Entrepreneur is

---

[27] J. Morgan, H. Orzen, M. Sefton, and D. Sisak, 'Strategic and Natural Risk in Entrepreneurship: An Experimental Study', *Journal of Economics & Management Strategy*, 25 (2016), p. 421.

[28] Naude and Chiweshe, 'A Proposed Operational Risk Management Framework', p. 4.

[29] A. De Vany, and W. D. Walls, 'Uncertainty in the Movie Industry: Does Star Power Reduce the Terror of the Box Office?', *Journal of Cultural Economics*, 23 (1999), 285–318; R. E. Caves, *Creative Industries: Contracts Between Art and Commerce* (Cambridge, MA: Harvard University Press, 2000); D. Miller and J. Shamsie, 'Strategic Responses to Three Kinds of Uncertainty: Product Line Simplicity at the Hollywood Film Studios', *Journal of Management*, 25 (1999), pp. 97–116; Dempster, 'An Operational Risk Framework', p. 152.

[30] P. Courty and M. Pagliero, 'The Pricing of Art and the Art of Pricing: Pricing Styles in the Concert Industry', in Victor A, Ginsburgh and David Throsby (eds.), *Handbook of the Economics of Art and Culture Vol. 2* (1st ed.) (Amsterdam: North Holland, 2013).

[31] T. Sattersten, *Every Book Is a Startup* (Sebastopol, CA: O'Reilly Media, Inc., 2011).

not as common a term in the book industry as one might find in, say, the tech industry. In interviews with US booksellers, publishers, and freelancers, it became clear that 'entrepreneur' was not a term regularly used by individuals in the book industry, even when they readily admitted that technically they would fit within the 'entrepreneur' category. Their comments on which terms they use and why revealed that their terminology choices were rooted in the desire to appear professional, innovative, stable, legitimate, and intentional. To this end, interviewees chose various terms to describe this: business owner, founder, caretaker, contractor, editor, freelancer, designer, publicist, etc.

Business Owner

Many interviewees chose to categorise themselves as a 'business owner'. Some did so because they saw entrepreneurship as being innovative, and did not see their own work as innovative: 'I generally know what I'm doing and what I'm providing and my clients know what they're looking for. I'm not trying to come up with some new and unexpected service that I need to sell.'

Those offering services rather than products (such as freelancers) saw entrepreneurs as individuals offering products, and therefore did not include themselves in that category:

> I call myself a business owner. And I think that more precisely
> walks the line because I do think entrepreneurship is a little tied
> to the idea of products versus services. And freelancer has some
> potentially negative connotations and a bit of instability or
> something that's less settled. So I definitely choose to refer to
> myself as a business owner.

Caretaker

Some book industry entrepreneurs are hesitant to take credit as an 'entrepreneur' when they see entrepreneurship as a networked endeavour that does not rest solely on one person. For this reason, one interviewee chose the term 'caretaker' instead of 'entrepreneur' or 'business owner'.

Contractor

The quest for legitimacy and to be seen as a legitimate professional in their roles as entrepreneurs was a common thread in the terminology discussions. To this end, some chose the term 'contractor' as a way to legitimise their role: 'I often say I'm a contract copy editor because it sounds more formal than freelancer to be a contractor.'

Editor, Designer, Publicist, etc., vs. Freelancer

While some interviewees did use 'freelancer' as their preferred term, many freelancers preferred to specify their role as being in editorial, design, or publicity rather than generic freelancing because it did not seem as stable or legitimate to freelance: 'Freelancing just seems like a side gig. So I don't like it when people say that they're full time freelancing. Just that you're a professional editor. Yeah. Why do you need to quantify it?'; 'I think that there is a stigma around it [the term 'freelancer']. Because freelancer sounds unsteady, right?'

Entrepreneur

What, then, is an entrepreneur in the book industry, as perceived by entrepreneurs in the book industry? An entrepreneur is described as someone taking on financial risk in the hope of greater financial reward: 'I am an entrepreneur because in my heart that sort of means like somebody stepping out to make money. I feel like that is, I guess, what I'm doing.'

An entrepreneur is someone with a larger vision and mission:

> To succeed as an entrepreneur, you have to have a vision that you just won't let go of because it's not easy. And you've got to believe in that every single day. Every hour. I mean, every time you're working at ten at night, you still have to believe in it. I think it's a mission-focused lifestyle.

An entrepreneur is someone who does something new: 'I still see that as being an entrepreneur that we're doing something new, even though it's this industry that's centuries old.' An entrepreneur is also a leader, someone in charge: 'So I do see myself as an entrepreneur in my mind. It's anybody who's going out and starting a business or running a business, and they are actually in charge of this particular way. They are in charge of the whole breadth of business, all the different aspects.'

The responses about entrepreneurship terminology from interviewees revealed some underlying questions that often guided their answers.

How do we measure entrepreneurial success? Is successful entrepreneurship just about money and funding? If so, then most publishers, booksellers, and freelancers would not count themselves as entrepreneurs. The low-entry nature of the book industry does not require the same start-up economic capital as is required in other fields, which allows both easier and less risky entry into the book industry as an entrepreneur, and can make book industry entrepreneurs doubt their own legitimacy. Additionally, most publishers, booksellers, and freelancers never make the kind of money that entrepreneurs in other industries do; the initial financial risk is less, but so is the reward.

If the intention is for a business to always be a microenterprise or a small business, is it still entrepreneurship? Many book industry entrepreneurs have only modest goals for growth, and perhaps do not want to worry about the hassle or complexity of hiring employees: 'I think of entrepreneurs as somebody building something that they don't intend to always be just themselves.'

If it is accidental or not planned from the start of one's career, is it still entrepreneurship? As will be discussed further in Chapter 1, the narrative of the accidental stumbling into the book industry is a common one amongst book industry professionals (including entrepreneurs). This is rooted in the lack of university-level programmes focused specifically on the book industry and the continued emphasis on the apprenticeship model in the book industry. Thus, many people do not realise that book industry employment or entrepreneurship is even a possibility until they 'stumble' upon it.

Entrepreneurship as Identity

The theoretical lens I employ here is a sociological one that takes into account the heterogeneous variety of entrepreneurs and the contexts that shape them. Entrepreneurship is socially embedded,[32] and some of these contexts are particular (or, at least, particularly important) to the book industry. Earlier scholars of entrepreneurship approached this topic by trying to find the secret to entrepreneurial behaviour in the personality traits,[33] cognitive functions,[34] and behaviour of entrepreneurs[35] who were economically successful. More recent entrepreneurship scholarship has moved away from searching for a unified definition of what makes an entrepreneur, and instead moved towards considering entrepreneurs as complex individuals within complex networks of contexts that shape them.

I am less interested in defining who an entrepreneur is and speculating about what makes an entrepreneur because entrepreneurship is not innate to some people and foreign to others; anyone, if all inequalities, gatekeepers, and barriers were stripped away, could be an entrepreneur. This is clear from the theoretical shift in the field to consider both entrepreneurial agency and entrepreneurial contexts on research about entrepreneurship: 'Emerging now are alternative constitutive approaches that emphasise the different ways in which entrepreneurs

[32] C. G. Brush, A. de Bruin, and F. A. Welter, 'Gender-Aware Framework for Women's Entrepreneurship', *International Journal of Gender and Entrepreneurship*, 1 (2009), p. 9.

[33] H. Zhao & S. E. Seibert, 'The Big Five Personality Dimensions and Entrepreneurial Status: A Meta-analytical Review', *Journal of Applied Psychology*, 91 (2006), p. 259; J. R. Baum, M. Frese, and R. A. Baron, 'Born to Be an Entrepreneur? Revisiting the Personality Approach to Entrepreneurship', in *The Psychology of Entrepreneurship* (Psychology Press, 2014), pp. 73–98.

[34] R. A. Baron and T. B. Ward, 'Expanding Entrepreneurial Cognition's Toolbox: Potential Contributions from the Field of Cognitive Science', *Entrepreneurship Theory and Practice*, 28 (2004), 553–73; J. A. Katz and D. A. Shepherd, 'Cognitive Approaches to Entrepreneurship Research', Vol. VI of *Advances in Entrepreneurship, Firm Emergence and Growth* (Bingley: Emerald Group Publishing Limited, 2003).

[35] S. A. Shane, *A General Theory of Entrepreneurship: The Individual-Opportunity Nexus* (Cheltenham/Northampton, MA: Edward Elgar Publishing, 2003).

and their environments are co-created.'[36] Therefore, in addition to the actions, personality, and cognition of the entrepreneur, the contexts in which entrepreneurs operate shape the entrepreneurial process.

What is more interesting, then, is why people pursue entrepreneurship and how entrepreneurship factors into their personal identities. Entrepreneurship is already embedded in national identity in America through the narrative of the American Dream, which permeates many aspects of daily American life. Because career narratives are 'influenced by prevailing discourses',[37] the American Dream discourse factors into the career narratives of individual entrepreneurs. This is an important thing to take into consideration for the interview data used in this research.

Entrepreneurs have 'a unique identity' that motivates and guides behaviour in their roles. Interest in entrepreneurial identity has been growing within the entrepreneurship field.[38] This raises the question: Why do

---

[36] R. Garud, J. Gehman, and A. P. Giuliani, 'Contextualizing Entrepreneurial Innovation: A Narrative Perspective', *Research Policy*, 43 (2014), p. 1180.

[37] J. Duberley and M. Carrigan, 'The Career Identities of "Mumpreneurs": Women's Experiences of Combining Enterprise and Motherhood', *International Small Business Journal*, 31 (2013), p. 632.

[38] A. R. Anderson and L. Warren, 'The Entrepreneur as Hero and Jester: Enacting the Entrepreneurial Discourse', *International Small Business Journal*, 29 (6), 589–609; Cohen and Musson, 'Entrepreneurial Identities'; Down, *Narratives of Enterprise*; S. Down and J. Reveley, 'Generational Encounters and the Social Formation of Entrepreneurial Identity: "Young Guns" and "Old Farts"', *Organization*, 11 (2004), 233–50; S. Down and L. Warren, 'Constructing Narratives of Enterprise: Clichés and Entrepreneurial Self-identity', *International Journal of Entrepreneurial Behavior & Research*, 14 (2008), 4–23; S. Downing, 'The Social Construction of Entrepreneurship: Narrative and Dramatic Processes in the Coproduction of Organizations and Identities', *Entrepreneurship: Theory and Practice*, 29 (2005), 185–204; C. Essers and Y. Benschop, 'Enterprising Identities: Female Entrepreneurs of Moroccan or Turkish Origin in the Netherlands', *Organization Studies*, 28 (2007), 49–69; L. Warren, 'Negotiating Entrepreneurial Identity: Communities of Practice and Changing Discourses', *The International Journal of Entrepreneurship and Innovation*, 5 (2004), 25–35; T. J. Watson, 'Entrepreneurial Action, Identity Work and the Use of Multiple Discursive

entrepreneurs identify as entrepreneurs, and how does this impact their entrepreneurship? Occupational identities, also called work identities, are the increasing focus of attention in management research.[39] Anderson and Warren argue that the 'entrepreneurial identity' label 'is sufficiently malleable to allow practising entrepreneurs to employ it to build their own individualized identity'.[40]

Drawing on social identity theory,[41] there are some key aspects of identity that are important to understand in the context of entrepreneurial identity: 1) identity is a position within a social group, 2) individuals have multiple identities,[42] 3) identities are complex,[43] 4) identities are fluid, 5) identities are situational, 6) identities require work to maintain, and 7) identities are produced in dialogue and narratives.[44]

First, identity is a position within a social group. According to Tajfel, identity stems from membership in a social group 'together with the value and emotional significance of that membership'.[45] Identity is related to

Resources: The Case of a Rapidly Changing Family Business', *International Small Business Journal*, 27 (2009), 251–74; E. Hamilton, 'Entrepreneurial Narrative Identity and Gender: A Double Epistemological Shift', *Journal of Small Business Management*, 52 (2014), 703–12.

[39] D. Kärreman and M. Alvesson, 'Cages in Tandem: Management Control, Social Identity, and Identification in a Knowledge-Intensive Firm', *Organization*, 11 (2004), 149–75; N. Phillips, P. Tracey, and N. Karra, 'Building Entrepreneurial Tie Portfolios through Strategic Homophily: The Role of Narrative Identity Work in Venture Creation and Early Growth', *Journal of Business Venturing* Special Issue: Institutions, Entrepreneurs, Community, 28 (2013), 134–50.

[40] Anderson and Warren, 'The Entrepreneur as Hero and Jester', p. 605.

[41] H. Tajfel, 'Social Psychology of Intergroup Relations', *Annual Review of Psychology*, 33 (1982), 1–39.

[42] Essers and Benschop, 'Enterprising Identities'.

[43] Hamilton, 'Entrepreneurial Narrative Identity and Gender', p. 4.

[44] Down and Warren, 'Constructing Narratives of Enterprise', 4–23; Essers, and Benschop, 'Enterprising Identities'.

[45] H. Tajfel, 'Social Psychology of Intergroup Relations', *Annual Review of Psychology*, 33 (1982), p. 23.

connecting with categorizations, and identity is socially constructed. For example, race is a social construct without biological basis,[46] but Americans have used racial categories throughout the history of the United States to distinguish between in-group and out-group: us and them.[47] Similar arguments could be made about the social construction of gender, generational categories, religious groups, etc. To identify with something is to belong, but it comes with embedded cultural values attached to that identity. Thus, an identity such as 'entrepreneur' is only useful to an individual because it comes with cultural values attached and ties the individual to others who also see themselves as entrepreneurs. Down and Warren argue that 'identity is not located in the personality of the individual, but instead is constituted through interaction between the individual, society and culture'.[48] Additionally, personal identity is inextricably linked to collective (social group) identities. Examining identity as both personal and collective can be useful in deconstructing the 'relatively complex social construction' that is identity, including entrepreneurial identity.[49]

Second, individuals have multiple identities. Larson and Pearson highlight the allowance of multiple and competing constructions of the self: 'Rather than having neat, highly stable identities, individuals must manage or negotiate many different possibilities for reflexively defining the self.'[50] For example, Essers and Benschop study the intersection of three particular identities: gender, race, and occupational identities: 'Being female, Turkish or Moroccan, and entrepreneur at the same time requires various strategies to negotiate identities with different constituencies. These strategies of identity work vary in the degree of conformity.'[51] Hamilton[52] examines the relationship between gender identity and occupational identity. Holding multiple identities

---

[46] M. Gannon, 'Race Is a Social Construct, Scientists Argue', *Scientific American* (2016), 5 February.

[47] Tajfel, 'Social Psychology of Intergroup Relations'.

[48] Down and Warren, 'Constructing Narratives of Enterprise', p. 5.

[49] Anderson and Warren, 'The Entrepreneur as Hero and Jester', p. 603.

[50] Larson and Pearson, 'Placing Identity', p. 243.

[51] Essers and Benschop, 'Enterprising Identities', p. 49.

[52] Hamilton, 'Entrepreneurial Narrative Identity and Gender'.

at once, which overlap and intersect in various ways, is important to consider when studying any type of identity, including entrepreneurial identity.

Third, identities are complex. This complexity includes identities that are sometimes ambiguous and contradictory. The narratives used to construct these identities can also be contradictory.[53]

Fourth, identities are fluid. Identity is fluid because it changes throughout an individual's life and (as a social group) throughout history. Hamilton defined entrepreneurial identity as 'an identity that is not a "categorical essence" but something fluid in space and time and constructed in relation to others'.[54]

Fifth, identities are situational. The situational nature of identity indicates that identity is very personal and individual in how it is experienced, and therefore identity is impossible to separate from the context in which it is constructed, performed, and shaped. Morris et al. called entrepreneurial identity 'unscripted, unpredictable, and uncontrollable', which is why the richness of the identity 'lies in how it is personally experienced'.[55] Kondo reminds us that we cannot separate selves from contexts, such as where, how, and to whom the self was performed.[56] Anderson et al. discuss the situation of place, not only 'where identity is enacted', but for entrepreneurs, where they are 'socially situated' or 'belong'.[57]

Sixth, identities require work to maintain. To understand one's self is a basic human drive,[58] and this influences identity formation efforts. Alvesson,

[53] Hamilton, 'Entrepreneurial Narrative Identity and Gender', p. 707.

[54] Hamilton, 'Entrepreneurial Narrative Identity and Gender', p. 704.

[55] M. H. Morris, D. F. Kuratko, M. Schindehutte, and A. J. Spivack, 'Framing the Entrepreneurial Experience', *Entrepreneurship Theory and Practice*, 36 (2012), p. 11.

[56] Dorinne K. Kondo, *Crafting Selves: Power, Gender, and Discourses of Identity in a Japanese Workplace* (Chicago: University of Chicago Press 1990), p. 247.

[57] Anderson, Warren, and Bensemann, 'Identity, Enactment, and Entrepreneurship Engagement', p. 1560.

[58] A. Reed II, M. R. Forehand, S. Puntoni, and L. Warlop, 'Identity-Based Consumer Behavior', *International Journal of Research in Marketing*, 29 (2012), 310–21.

Ashcraft, and Thomas[59] discuss this effort of identity formation as 'identity work'. Other scholars have elaborated on the definition, details, meaning, and processes of identity work: 'In exploring entrepreneurial identity, we have found that identity is rather more than simply something we have, or just about who we are ... Rather, identity seems to be something that we do identity work to acquire. Once acquired, it can be worked to considerable advantage.'[60] Watson defined identity work as work that 'is often done to say "who we are not" as well as "who we are"',[61] which ties back to the first point about identity being embedded in social group dynamics and in-group/out-group delineations.

Finally, identities are produced in dialogue and narratives. Narratives give meaning and value to events,[62] mediate experiences,[63] and 'play a critical role in the process of sensemaking'.[64] Not only do identities draw on narratives, but 'we are always reinterpreting our identity, drawing on narratives available to us via our culture embedded in our social and historical context'.[65] By mobilizing particular narratives, individuals identify themselves.[66] This process of identification and sensemaking through narratives is contextually embedded and bound.[67]

Narratives are important in the performance of identity because we shape narratives in order to shape how other people see us, allowing us to

[59] M. Alvesson, K. Lee Ashcraft, and R. Thomas, 'Identity Matters: Reflections on the Construction of Identity Scholarship in Organization Studies', *Organization*, 15 (2008), 5–28.

[60] Anderson and Warren, 'The Entrepreneur as Hero and Jester', p. 603.

[61] Watson, 'Entrepreneurial Action', p. 266.

[62] O. Byrne and D. A. Shepherd, 'Different Strokes for Different Folks: Entrepreneurial Narratives of Emotion, Cognition, and Making Sense of Business Failure', *Entrepreneurship Theory and Practice*, 39 (2015), 375–405.

[63] Hamilton, 'Entrepreneurial Narrative Identity and Gender'.

[64] Byrne and Shepherd, 'Different Strokes for Different Folks', p. 376.

[65] Hamilton, 'Entrepreneurial Narrative Identity and Gender', p. 706.

[66] M. Alvesson and H. Willmott, 'Identity Regulation as Organizational Control: Producing the Appropriate Individual', *Journal of Management Studies*, 39 (2002), 619–44.

[67] Duberley and Carrigan, 'The Career Identities of "Mumpreneurs"'.

connect with others in particular ways. Sometimes this involves the use of cliches in narratives to secure a particular identity.[68] Some of these clichés are tied to the enterprise culture in the United States, where the American Dream promotes upward mobility 'available to everyone through entrepreneurship'.[69] Down and Warren discuss representation of the entrepreneur 'as a mythical or heroic figure valorised to affect economic betterment for all'. Stereotypes and clichés such as these are all part of the cultural narrative surrounding entrepreneurship, which highlights key characteristics of entrepreneurs 'such as bravery, ambition, success, autonomy and self sufficiency that might be emulated and acquired through processes of identity work'.[70]

Entrepreneurial identity is a narrative construction, and a narrative approach and methodology is becoming more common in the academic space in order to explore entrepreneurship.[71] The interest in this

---

[68] Down and Warren, 'Constructing Narratives of Enterprise'; Down, *Narratives of Enterprise*.

[69] Down and Warren, 'Constructing Narratives of Enterprise', p. 5.

[70] Down and Warren, 'Constructing Narratives of Enterprise'.

[71] C. Bjursell and L. Melin, 'Proactive and Reactive Plots: Narratives in Entrepreneurial Identity Construction', *International Journal of Gender and Entrepreneurship*, 3 (2011), 218–35; L. Foss, '"Going Against the Grain ..." Construction of Entrepreneurial Identity Through Narratives', University of Illinois at Urbana-Champaign's Academy for Entrepreneurial Leadership Historical Research Reference in Entrepreneurship (2004); Cohen and Musson, 'Entrepreneurial Identities'; E. Hamilton, 'Whose Story Is It Anyway? Narrative Accounts of the Role of Women in Founding and Establishing Family Businesses', *International Small Business Journal*, 24 (2006), 253–71. U. Hytti, 'New Meanings for Entrepreneurs: from Risk-Taking Heroes to Safe-Seeking Professionals', *Journal of Organizational Change Management* (2004); Watson, 'Entrepreneurial Action'; I. Fillis, 'Biographical Research as a Methodology for Understanding Entrepreneurial Marketing', *International Journal of Entrepreneurial Behavior & Research*, 21 (2015), 429–47; D. Hjorth and C. Steyaert, *Narrative and Discursive Approaches in Entrepreneurship: A Second Movements in Entrepreneurship Book*, University of Illinois at Urbana-Champaign's Academy for Entrepreneurial Leadership Historical Research

methodology is growing so much, in fact, that Fletcher called it the 'fifth movement in entrepreneurship research'.[72] This narrative approach views entrepreneurship as not fixed or static, but dynamic in terms of how it is constantly shaped and constructed and reconstructed. This moves away, then, from trying to explain, predict, or generalise about the entrepreneurial experience, and instead towards investigating how entrepreneurial processes are 'socially constructed through language'.[73] Ultimately, these narratives 'assist in understanding what motivates individual entrepreneurs and how their businesses operate'.[74]

Methodology

While entrepreneurship is not limited to small business, it is often in small businesses that entrepreneurship is most visible. The US Small Business Administration defines a small business as any business with fewer than 500 employees – which covers a large range of companies and almost all of the publishing industry, except for companies such as the Big Five[75] (soon to be

Reference in Entrepreneurship (2004); W. B. Gartner, 'Entrepreneurial Narrative and a Science of the Imagination', *Journal of Business Venturing*, 22 (2007), 613–27; J. Larty and E. Hamilton, 'Structural Approaches to Narrative Analysis in Entrepreneurship Research: Exemplars from Two Researchers', *International Small Business Journal*, 29 (2011), 220–37; R. Jones, J. Latham, and M. Betta, 'Narrative Construction of the Social Entrepreneurial Identity', *International Journal of Entrepreneurial Behavior and Research*, 14 (2008), 330–45; A. W. Johansson, 'Narrating the Entrepreneur', *International Small Business Journal*, 22 (2004), 273–93; Downing, 'The Social Construction of Entrepreneurship'; Down and Reveley, 'Generational Encounters'.

[72] D. E. Fletcher, 'Entrepreneurial Processes and the Social Construction of Opportunity', *Entrepreneurship & Regional Development*, 18 (2006), 421–40.

[73] Jones, Latham, and Betta, 'Narrative Construction of the Social Entrepreneurial Identity', p. 332.

[74] Fillis, 'Biographical Research as a Methodology for Understanding Entrepreneurial Marketing', p. 432.

[75] Penguin Random House, Simon and Schuster, Macmillan, HarperCollins, and Hachette.

Big Four)[76] trade publishers, as well as Pearson, Scholastic, Cambridge University Press, etc. Under this definition, even Sourcebooks is considered a small business. The focus of this book is primarily on entrepreneurship in small business not only because of the visibility of entrepreneurship within this space, but also because of the logistics of gathering data from business owners within the publishing industry, the majority of whom own and manage small businesses.

There has been very little research on entrepreneurship in the book publishing industry, despite the fact that multimedia conglomeration and consolidation of book publishing in the twenty-first century has caused start-up small presses to emerge and encouraged publishers to 'externalise' labour and cut costs by turning previously salaried, full-time, in-house jobs into freelance work. Additionally, conglomeration and consolidation have caused a polarizing effect for company size in the United States; while the market is dominated by megacompanies, this has allowed a space for small companies to flourish as well.[77] The main research question this book aims to answer is this: How do entrepreneurs in the US book industry utilise narratives to frame and construct entrepreneurial identity?

In order to address this main question, there are several sub-questions that must be asked:

- What does it mean to be 'independent' in publishing (i.e. an independent bookseller or independent publisher), and what is the value placed on being independent?
- How do entrepreneurs in book publishing both combat and engage with the public perceptions (good and bad) of various entrepreneurship avenues?
- How are freelancers different from and similar to other types of self-employment and entrepreneurship in book publishing?

---

[76] J. Milliot, 'Bertelsmann to Buy S&S for $2.2 Billion' *Publishers Weekly*, 25 Nov. 2020.

[77] S. Brown (ed.), *Consuming Books: The Marketing and Consumption of Literature* (London: Routledge, 2006).

- What is the connection between entrepreneurship and well-being in book publishing?
- How does geography influence entrepreneurship for book publishing in the United States?
- What is the decision-making process like for twenty-first-century book entrepreneurs?
- What is both lost and gained in book publishing entrepreneurship?
- How do book publishing entrepreneurs manage risk and uncertainty in navigating the industry?
- What are the individual entrepreneurial start-up narratives for various book publishing entrepreneurs?
- How does social capital and previous work experience/networking in traditional publishing relate to success as a book publishing entrepreneur?

To investigate the research questions, semi-structured interviews with thirty-nine entrepreneurs across three main categories in the book publishing industry (publishers, freelancers, and booksellers) were conducted in person, via Zoom, or via phone during 2019 and 2020. Participants were recruited via email. Interviewees were chosen through purposive sampling, using PubWest, IBPA, American Booksellers Association, and Editorial Freelancers Association directories as starting points. I also endeavoured to make the sample as geographically diverse as possible, so while Portland book publishing entrepreneurs are represented, they are not the majority. Interviewees were from Utah, Arizona, New York, Oregon, Vermont, North Carolina, Minnesota, Massachusetts, Ohio, California, Idaho, Pennsylvania, Washington DC, and Wisconsin. In addition to geography, I endeavoured to diversify the areas of specialization for freelancers (i.e. design, editorial, marketing, etc.). The majority of respondents (thirty-five of the thirty-nine) self-identified as women. The interview questions, recruitment copy, and general methodology was approved for this project by Portland State University's Institutional Review Board for research with human subjects.

Interviews are a type of narrative. As a method, they allow a researcher to explore the ways in which the interviewees rhetorically position themselves, with an emphasis on 'their description of their practices and processes rather than the practices and processes themselves'.[78] As Squires argues: 'These discursive positionings are both part of their practice . . . and [are] actively constitutive of those practices'.[79] Therefore, the interviews are narratives unto themselves, but then the discursive practices and rhetorical positionings that interviewees utilise are rooted in socially embedded cultural narratives of entrepreneurship as well. I examined the interview data on both of these levels by organizing the qualitative data in NVivo in order to conduct a content and narrative analysis.

As with any research project, the scope and methodological choices have limitations. One area of entrepreneurship in the book industry that is not covered in this book is self-publishing and the authorpreneur.[80] While an important and interesting topic, there isn't the time or the space to do it justice here. In addition to focusing on publishers, booksellers, and freelancers, I also conducted interviews with a select number of literary agents; it's worth noting that there are many other areas of entrepreneurship in the book industry not captured here: literary agents, scouts, publishing consultants, distributors, and wholesalers, for example. The focus of this book is on entrepreneurship within the national context of the United States. Because of the situated nature of identity, acknowledging and addressing the geographical situation of the interviewees and their narratives within the US book industry is highly important. However, many of the narratives employed by US book industry entrepreneurs are also used in other book industries. So while this book is intentionally situated within the US context, its relevance is not exclusive to the US book industry or audience.

---

[78] C. Squires, 'The Passion and Pragmatism of the Small Publisher', in G. Colby, K. Marczewska, and L. Wilson (eds.), *The Contemporary Small Press: Making Publishing Visible* (Basingstoke: Palgrave Macmillan, 2020), 199–218.

[79] Ibid.

[80] For more on this subject, see Stephen Brown and Anthony Patterson, 'Dante Leave Homer Without It: On Epics, Umbras and Authorpreneurs', in I Fillis (ed.), *Handbook of Entrepreneurship and Marketing* (Cheltenham/Northampton, MA: Edward Elgar Publishing, 2020); S. Brown, 'Harry Potter and the Fandom Menace', *Consumer Tribes* (2006): 177–93.

The book is organised into three chapters, with an additional Introduction and Conclusion. This introduction has given an overview of the perception, narrative, and experience of entrepreneurship in the United States, founded crucially in the narrative of the American Dream. It has also relayed the previous literature on entrepreneurship, particularly entrepreneurial identity, and made an argument for the importance of narrative within that identity as the basis for the chosen method (interviews) and corresponding methodological approach.

Chapter 1, 'Independence amidst Consolidation: Independent Publishers and Bookstores', focuses on five focal narratives to the small publisher and bookseller space: 1) the independent narrative, 2) place narratives, 3) the culture over commerce narrative, 4) the accidental profession narrative, and 5) risk narratives.

Chapter 2, 'Freelancers: Flexibility and Uncertainty as a Contractor', focuses on three focal narratives to the freelancer space in the book industry: 1) the (in)stability narrative, 2) the busyness narrative, and 3) the freedom narrative.

Chapter 3, 'Intersectionality and Entrepreneurial Identity', explores the ways that entrepreneurial identity intersects with identities of gender, race, sexuality, religion, neurodiversity, and ableism.

1 Independence amidst Consolidation: Independent Publishers and Bookstores

1.1 A Brief Introduction to the Book Industry Landscape

In addition to the particular characteristics of entrepreneurship within the geographic context of the United States, we must also consider the particular characteristics of entrepreneurship within the book industry. In the book industry, entrepreneurship is visible in publishers, booksellers, freelancers, authors, literary agents, scouts, and even distributors. Due to the consolidation and conglomeration of publishing companies, bookstores, and distributors since the 1960s,[81] the book publishing industry is highly polarised in terms of company size.[82] Thus, while large players dominate market share, an entrepreneurial undercurrent moves the industry along. In this way, the book industry is not much different from other creative industries (such as film and music) that have experienced similar disruptive conglomeration and consolidation.

In the twenty-first century, entering into the book industry is, in some ways, less financially risky than it has ever been. Especially for publishers, booksellers, and freelancers who forego physical office or retail space (with all the associated overheads) and run the company with few employees (often relying heavily on contract/freelance or volunteer work), the digital world of the book industry can support entrepreneurship at a low start-up cost. Many developments of the late twentieth and early twenty-first centuries have helped shape this environment: the developments in print-on-demand technology for shorter print runs (and backing by large distribution players such as Ingram[83]), ease of producing and publishing e-books, online retail environments, growing acceptance of digital copies for review, ease of selling used books on online platforms such as Amazon, etc. Outside funding/investment is not very common for book publishing

[81] S. Murray, 'Publishing Studies: Critically Mapping Research in Search of a Discipline', *Publishing Research Quarterly*, 22 (2006), 3–25.

[82] Brown, *Consuming Books*.

[83] Lightning Source was created by Ingram in 1997 and IngramSpark was created in 2013.

entrepreneurship compared to other industries, which necessitates low start-up costs. Of the 900 book publishing start-ups McIlroy examined since 1997, only 15 per cent received investment funding.[84]

The low-paying, overworking, New York-centric nature of the book industry puts major limitations on employment in the industry, often leading to the choice and/or circumstance that drives an individual to entrepreneurship. This is illustrated by new bookseller entrepreneurs who start bookstore businesses in a city that has not had regular access to a local bookstore and where rent is not as exorbitant as in NYC. Or by new publisher entrepreneurs who found publishing houses to serve local readers and authors. Or by freelancer entrepreneurs who want the freedom to set their own rates, clients, projects, and schedules.

In their revised communication circuit for the digital twenty-first century, Squires and Ray Murray identify freelancing and outsourcing as one of the main areas of change in the book industry over the recent decades and centuries. These authors discuss how the dismantling of traditional publishing workflows also made the corporate structure of the publishing house less cohesive: 'The result is a more fragmented and atomized work culture. Fledgling companies are more likely to be built as lean start-ups . . . Valuing a streamlined approach, such a model employs people only when a need for a certain skillset is demonstrated.'[85] There are, of course, advantages and disadvantages to the increase in freelancers, but that will be discussed in Chapter 2.

Disruption can be a catalyst for innovation, as has been particularly visible during the COVID-19 pandemic when sudden changes to processes and daily life during the lockdown forced the book industry to think in creative ways about how to still run bookstores, publishing companies, and freelance businesses. But COVID-19 is not the only example of disruption

---

[84] T. McIlroy, 'An Authoritative Look at Book Publishing Startups in the United States', 2017, http://thefutureofpublishing.com/new/wp-content/uploads/2017/01/BookPublishingStartups-McIlroy.pdf, p. 7.

[85] C. Squires and P. R. Murray, 'The Digital Publishing Communications Circuit', *Book 2.0*, 3 (2013), 3–23.

in the industry: the book industry is an industry of disruptions, which makes fertile ground for the innovation that is intrinsic to entrepreneurship. Watson identified personal and industry-wide disruptions as key moments for deliberate identity work, which can entail an occupational identity shift to entrepreneurship: 'when individuals find themselves in situations of crisis or breakdown in an aspect of their lives, the need for deliberate identity work becomes most apparent; a manager being faced with redundancy for example or an entrepreneur finding themselves bankrupt'.[86]

One crucial feature of the book industry – and one that is also evident in other creative industries – is that both cultural capital and economic capital influence entrepreneurship. Economic capital can of course be a motivating force for entrepreneurs who see the risk involved in entrepreneurship as an opportunity for big financial gains. But entrepreneurs in the book industry are also motivated by cultural capital, and in fact are often reluctant to admit that economic capital is a motivating factor for them at all. This phenomenon is captured quite nicely in this assessment of the book business by Miller:

> It is striking how frequently people will comment that the book business is just not what it used to be. With great regularity, members of the industry wistfully hearken back to a golden age when individuals entered this line of work because they cared about books, not money; when publishers engaged with writers, not bestseller lists; and when the American public supported the neighborhood bookseller, who worked so hard to make a living. However, if one actually tries to locate this bygone era, it keeps receding further and further into the past. The years that present-day book people look back on so fondly were not seen as particularly golden by those living through them. Instead, for more than a century, members of the book world have worried about compatriots who appear to treat books as interchangeable commodities rather than as unique carriers

---

[86] Watson, 'Entrepreneurial Action', p. 257.

of ideas. There have certainly been some significant changes
in the organization of the industry and in how book professionals experience their work during this time. But the
perception of a vocation in danger of losing its moral
bearings has remained remarkably consistent.[87]

There are many revealing sentiments reflected in this common discourse
in which the American public wishes for a mythical book industry past.
Seeing economic capital as a distasteful reason for entering the book
industry (even though it is, after all, a business) is a clear one. Passion
does not pay bills, but this narrative is rooted in the idea that books as
cultural objects are different from other material goods. There is also the
assumption in this statement that personal relationships are at odds with
commerce (and with big publishers and bookstores). Finally, this statement
claims that hard work alone should warrant the support of readers.

The title of John Thompson's book about the twenty-first-century book
industry, *Merchants of Culture*,[88] is illustrative of the commerce and culture
connection too. There is a weightiness to the roles that book industry
professionals fill, and therefore entrepreneurs in the book industry feel
particularly motivated by (or at least *pronounce* that they are particularly
motivated by) the cultural power of the book industry, rather than any
economic promise such entrepreneurship holds.

Disruption, consolidation, cultural capital, low start-up costs,
New York geographical centricity, and an increase in freelancers all
characterise the twenty-first-century entrepreneurial environment in the
book industry. These factors shape entrepreneurial identities that come
across in five key narratives: the independent narrative, place narratives,
the culture over commerce narrative, the accidental profession narrative,
and risk narratives.

[87] L. J. Miller, *Reluctant Capitalists: Bookselling and the Culture of Consumption*
(Chicago: University of Chicago Press, 2006), p. 23.

[88] J. B. Thompson, *Merchants of Culture: The Publishing Business in the Twenty-First
Century* (Boston: Polity Press, 2012).

1.2 The Independent Narrative

Independent booksellers and independent publishers share many of the same characteristics, motivations, functions in the marketplace, and philosophies. Both booksellers and publishers are middlemen in a time when the digital literary sphere[89] is such that authors can reach readers directly if desired, without the assistance of publishers or booksellers. However, publishers and booksellers still add value to the book industry by providing editorial, design, and marketing work to shape and promote a manuscript, and to make that manuscript visible and accessible to a larger audience. Publishers and booksellers also act as gatekeepers and legitimizing forces in the industry, where getting a publishing contract with a publisher or seeing their book in a bookstore is often sought by the author as a means of legitimizing their work.

Both independent booksellers and independent publishers draw heavily on the discourse of 'independence' to frame their mission, value, and purpose. Both have been impacted by larger corporations in the industry (the Big Five publishers in New York, chain bookstores, Amazon) and have often sought to rhetorically position themselves in contrast to those larger corporations that hold greater market share and wield more financial power. Despite the many differences from independent publisher to independent publisher or independent bookstore to independent bookstore, there is a collective identity between independent publishers and independent booksellers that unites them. Despite differences in location, genre specialization, philosophy, business model, etc., being 'independent' unifies them.

In previous research, I argued that the vague, rhetorical use of 'independent' in the book industry is focused around three main definitions: independent as economically independent, independent as small, and independent as embodying a particular philosophy. This philosophy is characterised as editorially driven, locally rooted, author friendly, diversity focused, relationship based, quality concerned, and community building.[90] Miller describes independence in bookselling as signifying smallness, being

---

[89] S. Murray, *The Digital Literary Sphere: Reading, Writing, and Selling Books in the Internet Era* (Baltimore: Johns Hopkins University Press, 2018).

[90] R. Noorda, 'The Discourse and Value of Being an Independent Publisher', *Mémoires du livre / Studies in Book Culture*, 10 (2019).

locally based, and being geographically limited. There is also a philosophy of culture over commerce: 'These independents see themselves, in contrast to chains, as devoted to books for their own sake rather than as a means to acquire monetary reward.'[91] The use of 'independent' in narratives from and about publishers and booksellers arose in the 1970s and has continued with fervour since then.[92] The narrative use of 'independent' is a direct reaction to the conglomeration and consolidation that was and still is happening in publishing and bookselling. Chain bookstores, bookselling in large supermarkets, multimedia and multinational publishing companies: all of these disruptions contribute to bigness on the one end, and anti-bigness from independent booksellers and publishers on the other end: 'A sensitivity to bigness also helps explain why, around this time, independents were coming to define Amazon as equivalent to the major chains. Independents were increasingly seeing their interests as being opposed to those of online-only booksellers.'[93]

The anti-bigness movement that Miller describes is not limited to the book industry. As Miller points out, bigness manifests in the twentieth and twenty-first centuries in dislike of impersonal big cities and distrust of large organizations. The small business is seen as the heroic contrast to villainous bigness: 'small-scale enterprises, which could evoke if not exactly replicate the small community, lay the hope for maintaining a virtuous and free citizenry'.[94] On the one hand, concentrated ownership, such as has happened in the book industry, can be troubling in that, if we extend the metaphor of booksellers and publishers as gatekeepers, the keys to the gates are available to fewer and fewer people and organizations. Murray asks, 'If an ever-smaller number of firms controls most access points to publication and competes to supply a mainstream market with imitative bestsellers, how will genuinely innovative writing break through to find its readership?'[95]

[91] Miller, *Reluctant Capitalists*, p. 165.

[92] Miller, *Reluctant Capitalists*.

[93] Miller, *Reluctant Capitalists*, p. 182.

[94] Miller, *Reluctant Capitalists*, p. 15.

[95] S. Murray, *Introduction to Contemporary Print Culture: Books as Media* (London: Routledge), p. 58.

For example, the announcement of the purchase of Simon & Schuster by Penguin Random House at the end of November 2020 drew criticism from the Authors Guild:

> Less competition would make it even more difficult for agents and authors to negotiate for better deals, or for the Authors Guild to help secure changes to standard publishing contracts – because authors, even bestselling ones, wouldn't have many options, making it harder to walk away. The history of publishing consolidation has also taught us that authors are further hurt by such mergers because of editorial layoffs, canceling of contracts, a reduction in diversity among authors and ideas, a more conservative approach to risk-taking, and fewer imprints under which an author may publish.[96]

There are genuine questions and concerns regarding the vertical and horizontal integration that has been taking place in the book industry. And, similarly, there are truths to the claims of independent publishers and booksellers, such as a less hierarchical structure based on the small number of employees (if any) and constrained budgets.[97] The main difference between the book industry and other industries in their approach to anti-bigness is that publishers and booksellers readily use the 'independent' narrative alongside and/or in place of a 'smallness' narrative. 'Independent' is often used synonymously with 'small' in the industry, yet its connotations of radicalness, autonomy, quality, community, and personal attention are all wrapped up in this narrative and terminology. Whether or not it is always true that publishers who use the term 'independent' are actually able to publish more books that are diverse or of a higher editorial value and quality is not only difficult to measure, but also beside the point. The purpose of the narrative is to construct and maintain

---

[96] Authors Guild, 'AG Statement on Proposed Sale of Simon & Schuster and Its Ramifications for Authors'.

[97] Murray, *Introduction to Contemporary Print Culture*, p. 97.

identity for entrepreneurs as publishers and booksellers and for them to use rhetorically in order to shape perception of themselves and their businesses.

A publisher interviewee described how they saw their independent publishing house in contrast to the large houses: the Big Five.

> Until I learned about any publishing, knowing that the Big Five were so big and dominant was intimidating. But then I learned about all the infrastructure that's available that supports indie publishing. Here's an example: I was speaking to a literary agent who said, 'You know, you're at a disadvantage because if I have a client, I'm more likely to take them to the Big Five.' And it's true that the Big Five have an infrastructure that I don't have and resources that I don't have. But for me, I bring expertise about my community, and I feel that is an advantage over the Big Five.

In this quote, it's evident that the philosophy of being community-oriented and locally rooted is primarily how this publisher distinguishes themselves from larger publishers, acknowledging that this has a perceived value that is missing from larger corporations.

The independent narrative contributes to what Thompson calls the 'economy of favours'.[98] While large businesses in the book industry benefit from economies of scale due to the sheer numbers of books that they are producing and selling each year, small businesses in the book industry often benefit from the 'economy of favours'. Thompson describes the economy of favours thus:

> Small presses commonly share knowledge, expertise and contacts with one another. They see themselves as part of a common vocation and shared mission. Their competitive rivalries are overshadowed by the affinities that stem from their common sense of purpose, their shared understanding

---

[98] Thompson, *Merchants of Culture.*

of the difficulties faced by small publishers and their collective opposition to the world of the big corporate houses.[99]

One bookseller interviewee discussed the robust way that their independent bookshop had partnered with other small businesses and had drawn upon the generosity given to those who employed the independent narrative. This bookstore had partnered with many different local businesses, from yoga studios to running stores, to help build their network and to connect small businesses in sharing a common goal and philosophy. One of the ways that the bookshop was able to get off the ground was due to the generosity – economy of favours – of the company renting out retail space. Given that it was a newly constructed space in which the company was hoping to create a new area of the city that customers would be drawn to, the retail space company gave free rent for many months to the independent bookstore as a way to support the small business in the hopes that it would also attract people to the location, which it did. The interviewee spoke about the importance of community to the independent bookstore, saying, 'An independent bookstore is reflective of its physical community'.

1.3 Place Narratives

That particular bookseller's claim that 'an independent bookstore is reflective of its physical community' is a perfect transition into a series of narratives of publisher and bookseller entrepreneurs: place narratives. As we saw in the independent narrative, the locality and geographical community of the publisher or bookseller is a key part of the independent philosophy, which is why Miller described independence in bookselling as being 'locally based' and 'geographically limited'. The sheer size of the United States combined with uneven patterns of settlement results in a diverse geographical, cultural, and political space that varies from state to state. The Western US, which experienced European colonization much later than the Eastern US, is, in general, more sparsely populated, except for growing coastal urban centres, particularly in California.

---

[99] Thompson, *Merchants of Culture*, p. 156.

Place shapes occupational identity such as entrepreneurship.[100] In their study of entrepreneurs in Montana, Larson and Pearson[101] found three prominent discourses in which entrepreneurs framed their entrepreneurship in the context of place: place as lifestyle, place as home, and place as challenge. Because many of the publishers and booksellers interviewed for this research were geographically located outside of the American publishing hub of New York City, Larson and Pearson's narratives of place as lifestyle, place as home, and place as challenge can be seen in the narratives in the book industry as well.

For place as lifestyle, Larson and Pearson characterise Missoula as providing lifestyle advantages, such as better work–life balance, outdoor activities, arts, education, etc. Therefore, the portrayal of the ideal entrepreneur for this particular outside-NYC place is more balanced, in contrast to the typical ideal entrepreneur portrayal as being perpetually busy and a workaholic (discussed more in Chapter 2). Larson and Pearson did find that sometimes these narratives created challenges and internal conflicts for entrepreneurs to reconcile.[102] This 'place as lifestyle' identity also allows for intersectionality: it 'provides a resource to organize other facets of social identity during identity work'.

For place as home, Larson and Pearson found that there was a desirability and nobility 'to returning to the place where one was raised or where family resides to raise a family'.[103] The geographical flexibility of entrepreneurship affords individuals the opportunity to embrace place as home, which is what many book industry entrepreneurs do. This factors into a larger narrative of home and family.

For place as challenge, Larson and Pearson found that entrepreneurs framed their location in Montana as a challenge since it was not in the centre of booming industries (such as tech in Silicon Valley) and therefore presented more obstacles to success. This was also a narrative that came

---

[100] Larson and Pearson, 'Placing Identity'; Anderson, Warren, and Bensemann, 'Identity, Enactment, and Entrepreneurship Engagement'.

[101] Larson and Pearson, 'Placing Identity'.

[102] Larson and Pearson, 'Placing Identity', p. 252.

[103] Larson and Pearson, 'Placing Identity', pp. 253–4.

through in the book industry entrepreneur interviews, where some found it difficult to network, to have their books seen or recognised, or to attract attention from media and readers when they were geographically distant from the NYC industry hub. In addition to the place as lifestyle, place as home, and place as challenge narratives, I would add two others from the book industry: place as cultured, and place as entrepreneurial.

The place as cultured narrative is closely linked to the general narrative of cultural value being more important than economic value in the book industry. Therefore, a place with 'culture' is even more important than one with economic benefits. One interviewee described their location as 'not a publishing mecca, but intellectual', including 'a lot of good brain power'.

The cultured nature of place factored into the general perception of independent publishers and presses as well: 'The way that people see independent publishers or small presses over there. There's a little bit more of this kind of elitism, whereas over here on the West Coast (and maybe the whole country except for New York), it's more accepting.' In speaking about location in St. Louis, one interviewee talked about the city as an 'extraordinarily literary city' and one with 'fertile ground' that is 'still growing'. The interviewee commented that they didn't know if it would have been possible for them to found a publishing company anywhere else. If they hadn't been situated in such a cultured, literary place, the thought might never have occurred to them. But through the course of the interview, the interviewee challenged their own assumption about this. Would they have thought to start a publishing company if they had been located somewhere else? 'Arts are everywhere,' they eventually said. 'Sometimes you have to look to find them. Where there are people, there are writers and readers and storytellers. And I guess if you're determined enough, you'll find them and they'll find you.'

For place as entrepreneurial, this discourse saw the clustering of small businesses – not necessarily related to the book industry – as an important part of entrepreneurial identity and success. One bookseller talked about being in the heart of downtown: 'And it's almost all independent local businesses down here.' This bookseller, like many of the other booksellers I spoke with, frequently partnered with other independent businesses and made an effort to suggest to customers that they frequent other independent stores in the area. A publisher talked about the entrepreneurial spirit of Portland, particularly in the '90s, saying that the 'culture really influenced me to take it [starting a business] seriously. For everybody around me, entrepreneurship was their passionate art form. That was what they wanted to do, whether it was being an actor, making music. They would have some entrepreneurism as a clever way to make money that didn't require a lot of capital.' This entrepreneurial environment was a catalyst to showing this publisher that entrepreneurship was achievable and possible. Another publisher discussed purposefully enjoying being a 'bigger fish in a smaller pond' outside of the NYC publishing hub – having a place to thrive entrepreneurially in a location where the industry competition was not as fierce.

Place is a large and important narrative of entrepreneurship, with several sub-narratives. These narratives reveal how those entrepreneurs outside of the US NYC publishing centre identify as separate from NYC and as connected to each other. These narratives also reveal the various reasons why these entrepreneurs choose a particular location: to align with a preferred lifestyle, to return home, to conquer a challenge, to immerse in culture, and to find an entrepreneurial hub.

1.4 The Culture over Commerce Narrative

The 'culture over commerce' narrative permeates the book industry. What is most interesting about this narrative is that commerce is vitally important in the book industry, much like how culture and cultural capital are essential in other industries outside of the book industry. But entrepreneurs in the book industry use the rhetorical power of an appeal to culture over commerce to win customers, build a persona, and construct their own identities. Miller called culture and commerce 'conflicting visions' of how individuals collectively and individually benefit from products – particularly books.[104] The assumption underlying the culture over commerce narrative is that culture and commerce are fundamentally at odds with each other; yet the book industry demonstrates the importance of commerce and culture working together:

[104] L. J. Miller, *Reluctant Capitalists: Bookselling and the Culture of Consumption*, p. 6.

> Books, as storehouses of ideas and as a perceived means to human betterment, have long been viewed as a kind of 'sacred product' ... the organizations that constitute the book industry are not unique among for-profit enterprises in situating economic processes in social and cultural considerations. But what is unusual is that in the book industry, ambivalence to prevailing ways of organizing commerce tends to be made quite explicit.[105]

There are two primary ways in which the book industry narratively positions itself in the culture over commerce narrative. One is by downplaying business skills or the importance of the commerce side, and the other is by emphasizing passion.

1.4.1 Downplaying Commerce

While commerce is essential to the book industry, it is often portrayed as a necessary evil rather than something to be embraced. This perspective is particularly portrayed by small businesses/entrepreneur publishers and booksellers.

'I really hate the business side,' one interviewee admitted. Another acknowledged the need for commerce, but that it was not the focus of their business: 'You've got to promote yourself, your brand, your products. And I don't do that very well. I'm a book nerd. I like playing with books. I like it. I like working with other writers who are nerds. That's fun.' The specific terminology of 'book nerd' situates the entrepreneur within a community of readers who see themselves as bookish, as 'book nerds' rather than as part of a community of commerce.

Another interviewee took a more commerce-focused approach, but noted that this approach differed from many other small businesses in the book industry: 'There is a feeling like what I do is very different from what a lot of people here do, probably because I want to make money. And many of them probably don't make money or don't make a lot. But really, they

---

[105] L. J. Miller, *Reluctant Capitalists: Bookselling and the Culture of Consumption*, p. 19.

don't want to admit there's a vision of themselves as business people.' It's interesting that the simple desire and goal to make money – or, at least, to explicitly state that – was something that the interviewee did not see in others in the industry, almost as if commerce is the shameful secret that the book industry continues to incorporate but also de-emphasise in discourse.

1.4.2 Passion

Squires identifies passion as an important feature of small business in the book industry.[106] Cardon et al. note that not only is passion 'the experience of intense positive feelings' but, most importantly, 'these feelings are experienced for activities that are central to the self-identity of the individual.'[107] Thus, there must be a deep identity connection in addition to those intense feelings for passion to be a driving force. Passion is a driving force of entrepreneurship, promoting creativity and discovery of opportunities. For this reason, Cardon et al. note that passion is 'at the heart of entrepreneurship'.[108]

If passion necessitates 'activities that are central and meaningful to an individual's self-identity',[109] then we see a connection here with the identity of book industry entrepreneurs as readers. We might even consider thinking of book industry entrepreneurs as akin to user entrepreneurs because of the way in which they are immersed in their communities and create products that they would like to see in their own communities.[110] The identity as a reader is embodied in this particular quote from an interviewee: 'It was like writing and reading. It's always been a part of my life. Probably

---

[106] Squires, 'The Passion and Pragmatism of the Small Publisher'.

[107] M. S. Cardon, D. A. Gregoire, C. E. Stevens, and P. C. Patel, 'Measuring Entrepreneurial Passion: Conceptual Foundations and Scale Validation', *Journal of Business Venturing*, 28 (2013), 375.

[108] Cardon, Gregoire, Stevens, and Patel, 'Measuring Entrepreneurial Passion', 373–96.

[109] Ibid.

[110] P. P. Oo, T. H. Allison, A. Sahaym, and S. Juasrikul, 'User Entrepreneurs' Multiple Identities and Crowdfunding Performance: Effects through Product Innovativeness, Perceived Passion, and Need Similarity', *Journal of Business Venturing*, 34 (2019), 105895.

because generally I was a nerdy kid, you know. And so books were the one place where I could be, where it was okay to be the nerd. They weren't making fun of me.'

Key to their biographical narratives was a history with books since childhood, solidifying identities as readers. This manifested in various ways. One interview talked about libraries as the gateway to readerly identity:

> But I grew up in libraries. My mother is a retired librarian;
> she got her master's in library science when I was in school,
> in high school. And she worked in the library. And so we'd
> go from school to the library and just stay there until the end
> of the workday, and then go home and the books are just
> a part of that.

Because of this identity as a reader, entrepreneurship is fuelled by a passion for books that connects with individual identity. The notoriously low-paying nature of the book industry, in some ways, requires passion in order to sustain an entrepreneurial vision. One interviewee put it this way: 'As we all know, it's not like a high-margin industry. You know, there are other ways you can make a lot more money. But passion fuels things.' Another interviewee stated that passion was the key to entrepreneurship in the industry: 'I think it would be hard to do it without that passion.'

1.4.3 #BooksAreEssential Example

In April 2020, *Publishers Weekly* launched a social media campaign, 'Books Are Essential', that was promoted with the corresponding hashtag #booksareessential.[111] This came in response to the COVID-19 pandemic. As businesses, schools, and other organizations were forced to close starting in mid-March in the United States, the political rhetoric around which

---

[111] C. Cassidy, 'Publishers Weekly Launches #BooksAreEssential: Hashtag Campaign to Support Publishing Industry in Face of Covid-19', *Publishers Weekly* (20 April 2020).

organizations were deemed necessary to stay open centred upon whether they were 'essential' services or products.

This was a terrifying time for many bookseller and publisher entrepreneurs. Not only did the ones with physical retail space (booksellers particularly) have to close up shop or find alternative methods of selling in-store, such as kerbside pickup, but small publishers and booksellers have a long history of not having self-sufficient online selling mechanisms of their own. This is related to brand recognition, which is much more author-focused than publisher- or bookshop-focused. While small publishers and booksellers usually have websites through which they can sell books, these websites are not the primary avenue via which customers buy their books. In this environment, they were reliant on Amazon. However, Amazon was overwhelmed by the influx of customers, especially at the start of the shutdown, and announced that they would be selling and shipping only essential products (medical supplies, food, etc.) until further notice.

With no way to personally and physically connect with customers, and with mega online bookselling platform Amazon deeming books nonessential, the publishing industry's response was embodied in the *Publishers Weekly* 'Books Are Essential' campaign. The initiative was not without its critics.[112] Interestingly, this argument is an old one, tied to the cultural and symbolic value of books. Perceiving and portraying books as different to other products because of their cultural importance has long been the narrative of the industry. Small publishers and booksellers capitalise on this narrative even more so than the larger players in the industry.

1.5 The Accidental Profession Narrative

During their interview, one book industry entrepreneur discussed the term 'entrepreneur' and why they did not see it used often: 'I think it's also the industry. I think there's a lot of people who would be categorised as entrepreneurs, but they don't see themselves in it, and maybe that's because of the kind of accidental way that a lot of people come in.' The narrative of the accidental profession is manifest in many ways: starting a business as

---

[112] E. Hane and L. Zats, 'Letter to the Editor: Why These Agents Argue Books Aren't Essential', *Publishers Weekly*, 28 April 2020.

a hobby, perceiving and projecting being a book industry entrepreneur as a calling or mission (as inevitable), and framing entrepreneurship in the book industry as a second career.

In her research on book industry entrepreneurs in the Pacific Northwest, Ramdarshan Bold titled her article 'An Accidental Profession'. In the article, she equates this 'accidental profession' with publishing as a hobby:

> This idea of publishing as a hobby, an 'accidental profession', instead of a business is one that characterises a couple of the publishers interviewed for this research: particularly those based in Portland and Seattle . . . Several of the other publishers started out 'accidentally' or as a 'hobby': turning professional has changed their attitudes towards what they publish.[113]

The accidental profession narrative comes with various characteristics. Embedded here are some elements of narratives previously discussed regarding passion and culture over commerce. After all, the accidental profession narrative is tied to the idea that success and rewards for entrepreneurship are not just financial. In her study of small publishers in the UK, Squires notes that

> the idea of the hobbyist publisher is one worth further consideration. It connects to the idea of passion-led publishers, with one owner-manager describing her operation as having to 'be a passion, I think, because it's a shrinking industry'. Such language suggests that the rewards from their publishing are derived from aspects other than the financial.[114]

---

[113] M. R. Bold, 'An "Accidental Profession": Small Press Publishing in the Pacific Northwest', *Publishing Research Quarterly*, 32 (2016), 84–102.

[114] Squires, 'The Passion and Pragmatism of the Small Publisher'.

Noting the importance of passion and of motivators other than financial reward is not only key to understanding publisher and bookseller entrepreneurs, but entrepreneurs in other industries too. Baumol, Litan, and Schramm reveal that typically, entrepreneurs earn less money than their employee counterparts. Which, of course, raises the question: Why would entrepreneurs engage in such work, then? 'Because the additional rewards – being one's own boss, pride in self-accomplishment, and so forth – make the entrepreneurial endeavor worthwhile even if the entrepreneur does not gain the mega-prize.'[115] Miller describes what this looks like for booksellers:

> People who choose to run an independent bookstore are generally deeply committed to their enterprises; except in the rarest of cases, there is little money to be made, and long hours and tremendous uncertainties are the norm. Independent booksellers consistently describe their work as more than just a way to make a living, and more than just a means of escaping the constraints that come from working for somebody else. These booksellers see themselves as bettering society by making books available.[116]

The accidental profession narrative tells a story of entrepreneurial pursuits in the book industry as an inevitable calling or mission. One interviewee described it as falling into a profession that was meant to be: 'And I just happened to one day stumble upon the publishing part of it. Yes. I really felt like it was exactly what I wanted to do.' Another interviewee described this career trajectory as being called into a place of belonging: 'I like books. I had to know almost that it was a calling for me, that this is where I belong.' Thus, entrepreneurial pursuit in the book industry is framed as a journey of self-discovery, identification, and belonging. Because of their identities as readers, book industry entrepreneurs described

---

[115] Baumol, Litan, and Schramm, *Good Capitalism, Bad Capitalism*, p. 87.
[116] Miller, *Reluctant Capitalists*, p. 14.

their places in this industry as inevitable, as if there was an invisible force pulling them towards it.

Despite the use of the word 'accidental' in these narratives, they do not frame entry into the book industry as an accident in terms of a mistake, but rather as an unintended but welcome outcome. In this way, we can see the 'accidental profession' aligned with discussions of entrepreneurial serendipity. Dew defines serendipity as 'search leading to unintended discovery'[117] in which individuals are searching and 'accidentally discover something that they were not looking for.'[118] This is a narrative used by many prominent entrepreneurs (Dew gives Honda and Staples as specific examples) to frame the founding of businesses. In discussing a specific creative innovation in their company, one small publisher described it in terms of serendipitous creativity: 'We made our own publishing software. So I think we're going to have to start licensing it for other publishers. And that was all by accident: we didn't mean to do that.'

Entrepreneurship in the book industry was a second career for some, and even a third career for others. This, too, contributes to the narrative of inevitability in the book industry. While some individuals had chosen other careers in the beginning, various factors still lead them – inevitably – to books. There are, of course, other factors at play here: perhaps the low-paying and low-margins nature of the book industry contributes to entry into the book industry being a later career, one driven by passion after having established some financial security and economic capital.

1.6 Risk Narratives

Risk is considered a key feature of entrepreneurship.[119] As was discussed in the Introduction, there are five types of risk that are relevant to the creative industries (particularly publishing): financial, competitive, reputational,

---

[117] N. Dew, 'Serendipity in Entrepreneurship', *Organization Studies*, 30 (2009), 739.

[118] Dew, 'Serendipity in Entrepreneurship', p. 736.

[119] D. Carson, S. Cromie, P. McGowan, and J. Hill, *Marketing and Entrepreneurship in SMEs: An Innovative Approach* (New York: Pearson Education, 1995); M. Casson, B. Yeung, A. Basu, and N. Wadeson, *The Oxford Handbook of Entrepreneurship* (New York: Oxford University Press, 2008).

natural, and operational. Natural risk, also called 'luck' or 'serendipity', is the risk that, despite an entrepreneur's best decision-making and business practices, there is always an element of the 'accidental' to success. In the accidental profession narrative, publishing entrepreneurs spin the uncertainty of natural risk in a positive way by fashioning the luck and serendipity to reinforce the passion-led inevitability of their entrepreneurial paths. We all know that fluctuating trends in reading tastes, new fads and fashions in media consumption overall, and a myriad of other factors may morph and change without warning. The long production schedules for books (typically 12–18 months) leave plenty of room in the interim for market mutations to impact the product.

Beyond natural risk, entrepreneurs in publishing take chances in several ways. Financially independent publishers cover expenses such as the author's advance and distribution and marketing costs for the book; independent booksellers pay for physical retail space and inventory. All of these monetary costs are risks for publishers and booksellers because there is a chance that the books won't sell and the businesses won't be able to continue. Additionally, publishing is a very crowded marketplace,[120] with high competition for products. Therefore, independent publishers and booksellers must also manage competitive risk, or the risk associated with the decisions and actions of their competitors. Often these main sources of competition are seen as the largest players: Big Five publishers, chain booksellers, and Amazon. Operational risk is also a consideration for independent publishers and booksellers; one particular example of this is with returns. The returns policy in the publishing industry places 100 per cent of the risk on the publisher, who bears the burden of lost sales and extra inventory that can be returned from the retailer many months after initial purchase. The uncertainty and cash flow problems associated with this system can be catastrophic, particularly for small publishers.

Certainly, the narrative of independent publishers and booksellers portrays the small businesses in the book industry as facing greater risk in

---

[120] In 2019 the total number of books published in the United States exceeded 4 million, according to the ProQuest Bowker Report.

various ways: publishing or selling 'risky' authors with small audiences and minimal to no track records, focusing on diverse titles and authors with underserved audiences and underrepresented themes, and emphasizing 'quality' titles and genres in highbrow areas that typically move fewer copies. For the most part, these narratives revolve primarily around financial risk.

The industry is framed (often with good reason) as low-paying and with low margins. This in some ways makes entrepreneurial work in the book industry riskier than other industries because there is not the same prospect of high financial reward. One interview defined financial success as not losing too much money: 'So for the week we consider it really good if we don't lose too much money. I mean, it's like, you know, that's the budget. That's true for a lot of publishers.'

On the other hand, low entry costs to starting a publishing house or bookshop also help to lower financial risk. Costs are often personally funded, rather than sourcing investment from others. One interviewee relayed such a situation: 'Yeah, you know, I funded it out of our personal funds and I don't remember how much it was, but I used personal funds to start it up and then I had to continue to fund it for a while.' Even more interesting than how the risk in the book industry compares to other industries is how the narrative of risk is particularly strong for book industry entrepreneurs, in a way to set themselves apart from the larger organizations in the industry.

In her research on small publishers in the UK, Squires addresses the following question: are small publishers more or less risk averse than their larger counterparts? One editor told Squires that financially they 'can't really take the hit that some of the bigger houses can'. As Squires notes, 'This insight differs from a normative account, repeated by more than one publisher in my sample, that conglomerate publishers are "risk averse" whereas independents are not.' The dissonance between the common risk narrative of entrepreneurs in the book industry and the reality of small business financial constraints is evident here. The small size of entrepreneurial ventures in the book industry 'intensifies risk and can be a barrier to digital innovation and growth'. Thus, Squires argues that the risk is greater for small companies in the book industry, but that, contrary to the popular narrative, these book industry entrepreneurs are not taking risks like the larger organizations are. The financial cushion that larger companies have can allow these organizations to take those risks because they can 'amortise financial losses and successes across the company'[121]

Risk plays a part in entrepreneurial identity in the book industry because book industry entrepreneurs want to be seen as the ones taking risks (specifically financial risks) because that connotates greater innovation and perhaps breaking through some of the common publishing traditions and norms that have long been lamented, such as primarily supporting white, cis, straight authors and employees. The risk narrative exists because book industry entrepreneurs get value from being perceived as risk-takers in the industry, the ones charting new territory. But the reality is that financial assets and backing are important for providing the fallback cushion necessary for book industry organizations to take those risks, and economic capital is often in short supply for book industry entrepreneurs. Taking a risk on a particular author, book, etc., can sink a small entrepreneurial press or bookstore, and so while risk-taking is an attractive way to be perceived, it is a difficult undertaking in practice, with the possibility of truly disastrous results.

1.7 Support for Indies: The Case of Bookshop.org

This chapter has discussed the common entrepreneurial narratives of independent publishers and booksellers. Because context is essential to understanding entrepreneurship and entrepreneurial identity in a particular industry at a particular moment, the rising support for indies (based around many of the narratives discussed herein) can be seen in the example of Bookshop.org.

Bookshop.org was officially announced to the publishing industry at the American Booksellers Association Winter Institute in Baltimore in January 2020. Bookshop.org was launched shortly thereafter. The timing of Bookshop's launch could not have been more perfect, as the site launched only a few months before an unforeseen global event that no one in publishing anticipated: the COVID-19 pandemic. Suddenly, all

[121] Squires, 'The Passion and Pragmatism of the Small Publisher'.

brick-and-mortar bookstores, including independents, were unable to operate in their physical spaces for health and safety reasons. Many of these shops did not have the existing infrastructure of a discoverable and comprehensive website to move their bookstores into the online space. But Bookshop was already positioned to support independent bookshops and readers in the online space. As a result, sales at Bookshop soared at the same time that the virus did.[122] Andy Hunter, founder of Bookshop.org, said, 'If it's sticky and it lasts beyond this COVID crisis, it's going to really help bookstores thrive.'[123]

Before founding Bookshop.org, Hunter was the publisher and COO at the independent publisher collective Catapult, Soft Skull Press, and Counterpoint. Hunter founded Bookshop.org as a competitor to Amazon – the industry behemoth that independent publishers, booksellers, and many readers see as the epitome of bigness, commerce at the expense of culture, and ruthless commercialism. Bookshop.org operates on a model that gives 30 per cent of profits to independent bookstores – much more generous than the 10 per cent affiliate dividend that Amazon offers. Orders are fulfilled directly and shipped through the largest US book distributor, Ingram.[124] The sentiment against Amazon in the book industry is so strong that, in the media, Bookshop.org was characterised in Star Wars terms as the Rebel Alliance standing up to the Amazon Empire.[125]

Andy Hunter is himself described in the media as an entrepreneur,[126] and in metaphors such as that of the Rebel Alliance we see Bookshop being positioned as the heroic entrepreneurial enterprise that supports a collection

---

[122] E. Nawotka, 'Sales Skyrocket at Libro.fm and Bookshop.org', *Publishers Weekly* (16 March 2020).

[123] A. Alter, 'Bookstores Are Struggling. Is a New E-Commerce Site the Answer?' *The New York Times* (16 June 2020): www.nytimes.com/2020/06/16/books/bookshop-bookstores-coronavirus.html.

[124] Alter, 'Bookstores Are Struggling'.

[125] J. Warner, 'Bookshop.org Hopes to Play Rebel Alliance to Amazon's Empire', *Chicago Tribune* (15 January 2020).

[126] G. Lyons, 'An Indie Alternative to Amazon?' *Poets and Writers* (12 December 2019).

of other small businesses (independent bookshops). Bookshop.org has been similarly beneficial for small publishers. Publishers can make their own Bookshop.org pages and lists, and if customers order from those lists and pages, the publisher gets a percentage from Bookshop. Because of this, Bookshop.org has had the support of small, independent publishers and large publishers alike. Many Big Five publishers have pushed readers towards Bookshop too. Simon & Schuster CEO Carolyn Reidy said, 'Independent bookstores are a crucial link in the chain that brings authors to readers, and are a vital force in building and maintaining a sense of community in cities and towns across America.'[127]

In a letter introducing Bookshop to independent bookstores, Andy wrote the following:

> Like all of us who have made books the center of our lives, I have a deep and abiding love for bookstores, which I have known since childhood as places to find meaning. Books allowed me to discover myself and the world, and they still do. Bookstores are the physical roots of book culture, necessary for literature, ideas, our social conscience, and our understanding of ourselves and the world, and if we don't nurture and protect them, people won't simply find other places to get books, they'll read fewer books. Without your stores, books will become a smaller part of our culture, and that would be bad for individuals, society, and the future, which is already so fraught.

In this letter, Andy establishes his identity first and foremost as a reader, an identity that he claims to have had since childhood. This call for Bookshop is also a call for independent bookstores, and Andy makes it by evoking the many narratives that we have already discussed: small book-stores as having a philosophy that is location-based and community-serving, with entrepreneuring booksellers motivated not by profit but by

[127] J. Maher, 'S&S Partners with Bookshop.org', *Publishers Weekly* (31 March 2020).

the importance of books as a cultural force in the world. In this way, booksellers are framed as missionaries with a higher calling: to preserve cultural and literary space and heritage through the written word.

Bookshop.org is not the only collective combatting Amazon or fiercely demonstrating support for independent publishers and booksellers. Libro. fm is a similar rebelling force against Amazon's Audible in the independent audiobook industry, for example. But Bookshop.org is an interesting example of the narrative and support for independent bookshops (and publishers) during a particular context – the global pandemic of 2020. During 2020, Bookshop sold $51 million worth of books.[128]

As this chapter has illustrated, the book industry in the twenty-first century has been characterised by disruptions, including consolidation that has led to a polarised industry in terms of company size and entrepreneurial activity. The increase in freelancers, a geographical centre in New York, low start-up costs, and a focus on cultural capital all impact the narratives and entrepreneurial identities in the book industry. Five key narratives were discussed: the independent narrative, place narratives, the culture over commerce narrative, the accidental profession narrative, and risk narratives. The independent narrative positions the publisher and bookseller entrepreneur as autonomous, local, radical, and small (anti-big). Most importantly, the independent narrative is intertwined with the culture over commerce narrative, wherein independent publishers and booksellers are seen as caring more about cultural value than commercial value. This is portrayed in narratives by downplaying business skills or the importance of the commercial side and by emphasizing passion. The cultural nature of the book industry entrepreneur makes such efforts more of a calling or a mission that frames the career trajectory as an 'accidental profession' that led an individual inevitably into the industry where they were always meant to be. And although small publishers and booksellers bear more financial risk than their larger counterparts, because of this they are not able to take the same risks on new projects – contrary to the popular narrative of small publishers and booksellers as supporting innovation and taking on risks that the big companies will not.

---

[128] E. Nawotka, 'Bookshop and Libro Post Strong Sales in 2020', *Publishers Weekly* (8 January 2021).

2 Freelancers: Flexibility and Uncertainty as a Contractor

Freelancing is not often included in book industry entrepreneurship categories and discussions, but freelancing has been addressed in the entrepreneurship literature more broadly.[129] Much of the entrepreneurship literature on freelancing is focused on the gig economy, particularly on low-skilled workers and platforms such as Uber, eBay, Postmates, Amazon, and Airbnb (to name a few). But the book industry freelancer is different from these other workers in the gig economy because book industry freelancers tend to have a specialised skill set and are highly educated, sometimes with previous work experience as an employee within the industry in some capacity before moving to freelance work. While book industry freelancers are impacted by layoffs and underemployment, it is not necessarily a main determining factor in pursuing freelancing.

In the entrepreneurial literature, freelancers have sometimes been characterised as entrepreneurs,[130] hybrid entrepreneurs,[131] a type of small business owner,[132] solo self-employed,[133] and enablers of entrepreneurship

[129] G. Burtch, S. Carnahan, and B. N. Greenwood, 'Can You Gig It? An Empirical Examination of the Gig Economy and Entrepreneurial Activity', *Management Science*, 64 (2018), 5497–520.

[130] B. R. Mathisen, 'Entrepreneurs and Idealists: Freelance Journalists at the Intersection of Autonomy and Constraints', *Journalism Practice*, 11 (2017), 909–24; E. Salamon, 'Digitizing Freelance Media Labor: A Class of Workers Negotiates Entrepreneurialism and Activism', *New Media and Society*, 22 (2020), 105–22.

[131] D. Bögenhold and A. Klinglmair, 'Independent Work, Modern Organizations and Entrepreneurial Labor: Diversity and Hybridity of Freelancers and Self-Employment', *Journal of Management & Organization*, 22 (2016), 843–58.

[132] D. Smallbone and J. Kitching, 'Are Freelancers a Neglected Form of Small Business?' *Journal of Small Business and Enterprise Development*, 19 (2012), 74–91.

[133] N. de Vries, W. Liebregts, and A. van Stel, 'Explaining Entrepreneurial Performance of Solo Self-Employed from a Motivational Perspective', *Small Business Economics*, 55 (2020), 447–60; Burke and M. Cowling, 'The Role of Freelancers in Entrepreneurship and Small Business', *Small Business Economics*, 55 (2020), 389–92.

in small firms.[134] Freelancers in the book industry exist on a spectrum of entrepreneurship that is manifest in various ways. Some book industry freelancers also employ other freelancers, therefore operating with contractors like many small businesses, which would make the 'solo self-employed' category less applicable in such cases. Others work as freelancers by themselves. Some book industry freelancers are dedicated and focused on running their freelance work as a business, including business incorporation, business and marketing plans, etc. Others are not as comfortable with the business side of things, but still apply their specialised skill set to provide valuable services to the industry. But in all of these varied contexts of book industry freelancers, we can describe them as discovering, evaluating, and exploiting opportunities to create services: an entrepreneurial positioning.

While many scholars have focused on the 'choice' to become a freelancer, and on freelancers who chose such a path,[135] aligning with the embedded approach taken in this book that considers the contextual aspects of entrepreneurship, the interconnected nature of both choice and circumstance must be accounted for. Even for freelancers whose narratives explain their freelancing path as a choice, circumstances surround those choices. Part of the negative stigma associated with freelancing (even in the academic literature) has centred around portraying freelancers as unemployed or underemployed workers who were forced down a nontraditional and less desirable path. But, as recent research has shown, this is far from the truth. Especially in the book industry, freelancers utilise agency and autonomy in their pursuit of a freelance path. This agency and autonomy – much like the agency and autonomy of entrepreneurial pursuit more generally – is rooted and situated within the context of the social, cultural, economic, and political factors in which the individual operates.

Another aspect of the negative stigma associated with freelancing considers freelancing to be unethical: 'many companies are now reliant on

---

[134] Burke and Cowling, 'The Role of Freelancers in Entrepreneurship and Small Business'.

[135] J. Das, 'Sydney Freelance Journalists and the Notion of Professionalism', *Pacific Journalism Review: Te Koakoa*, 13 (2007), 142–60; Mathisen, 'Entrepreneurs and Idealists'.

a growing number of freelance workers; a precarity of the workforce that might be at odds with some aspects of ethical behaviour in business that independents might otherwise promote'.[136] Such a claim is not unfounded in the book industry, as there is a shift towards more freelance work[137] and freelancers do experience certain precarities that employees do not: for example, uncertainties of consistent work-flow and cash-flow; lack of healthcare, paid vacation time, and paid parental or sick leave; and the day-to-day concerns of running a business. However, freelancing in and of itself is not an unethical option in the industry. It is, instead, a question of ethics in terms of whether or not skilled book industry professionals are forced into freelance work because the industry offers no other options.

This chapter will focus on three narratives of book industry freelance entrepreneurship that emerged from the interview data. Some of these narratives are broadly applicable to freelance narratives beyond the book industry, while others are more industry specific. Given the limited research that has been done on entrepreneurship in the form of freelancing in the book industry (and in other industries), even the more broadly applicable narratives provide valuable insights to the scant research that exists on this subject. The narratives that this chapter will focus on are the (in)stability narrative, the busyness narrative, and the freedom narrative.

2.1 Employees vs Contractors

Many of the details of employment legislation are left up to individual states in the US, which means that conditions differ from state to state. Small publishers and freelancers in California were alarmed in January 2020 when the California Assembly Bill 5 (AB5) took effect in the state, for example. This bill requires employers to reclassify many contract workers as employees. The main push for the bill was to provide better and more stable conditions for workers in companies such as Uber, but the bill also had implications for the book industry. Being classified as an employee, rather than a contractor, requires more resources and money from the employer to supply overtime pay, sick leave, disability leave, unemployment insurance,

---

[136]   Squires, 'The Passion and Pragmatism of the Small Publisher'.

[137]   Squires and Murray, 'The Digital Publishing Communications Circuit'.

etc. When this bill became effective, many individuals and organizations in the book industry in California were worried it might discourage publishers from using freelancers and ultimately harm the industry.[138] Accordingly, 'some out-of-state publishers . . . stopped using California-based freelancers in order to avoid the burdens of the new law'.[139] However, as long as the freelancer worked on thirty-five projects or fewer per year with one employer, they would be exempt under the law. One interviewee had this to say about the bill:

> It's very complex because I think this legislation that is being passed and being looked at in California is extremely danger- ous for people who do freelance work and contract work and not as effectively catching the businesses that are just refusing to hire employees. I understand the attempt and I appreciate that Uber is not supporting employees like employees, but going about it this way, I think, is a little bit dangerous because there's a growing number of freelancers, people my age [millennials] who don't have the same job stability. So it kind of fell on our shoulders to ensure that we're going to be taken care of, not our employers. And taking away that freedom to manage our livelihood like that is pretty frustrat- ing. Further freelancing in especially remote work allows you to find the person that you need, not just the person you like. There's a very big difference in skill set and qualifications. And if you are strictly stuck with what's local, it's going to change the results. I don't think there are very many situ- ations where you have to be in a room with a person to get a job done. And if you let people work in situations where they can be their best, they'll do their best. And freelancing usually provides that . . . I literally can't see a downside to

[138] J. Boog, 'Publishers Brace for California Labor Law Changes', *Publishers Weekly* (17 December 2019).

[139] J. Kirsch, 'California's New Labor Law, AB-5, and What It Means for Publishers', Independent Book Publishers Association (17 January 2020).

using freelancers and contractors, except that it makes some
people who are used to other methods uncomfortable.

The controversy and implications associated with the California Assembly
Bill 5 reinforces the employee–contractor dichotomy that exists within
categorizations of types of workers in the United States. The Editorial
Freelancers Association issued a statement about the bill, expressing concern
specifically about its reclassification of independent contractors as
a 'fundamental misunderstanding of how an independent contractor functions
in our economy'. The EFA goes on to say: 'For many of our members,
functioning as an independent contractor/freelancer is more profitable,
flexible, and secure than traditional employment. The autonomy of operating
as an independent contractor is essential to many of our members.'[140]
Another law that has prompted discussion and debate in the book
industry and elsewhere is the Protecting the Right to Organize (PRO)
Act. The PRO Act would permit collective bargaining and unionizing from
freelancers, which is currently in violation of antitrust laws. The Authors
Guild has shown strong support for the PRO Act.[141] However, other
freelance organizations, including the Editorial Freelancers Association,
have raised concerns about aspects of the Act, such as the ABC classification
test that would prohibit most independent contractors from working with
clients.[142] In March, the PRO Act passed the vote in the US House of
Representatives and, at the time of writing this book, has not yet seen
a decision from the US Senate.

2.2 The (In)Stability Narrative

In positioning their own narratives about freelancing, book industry freelancers necessarily engage with narratives and perceptions about

---

[140] 'Statement on Legislation Affecting Freelancers', Editorial Freelancers
Association. www.the-efa.org/statement-on-legislation-affecting-freelancers/
[141] E. Nawotka, 'Authors Guild Asks Members to Support PRO Act', *Publishers
Weekly* (1 April 2021).
[142] C. Frey and B. Keenan, 'EFA Statement on the PRO Act', Editorial Freelancers
Association.

freelancing more generally. Despite the growth in freelancing in the book industry,[143] freelancing in the media industries and creative industries overall,[144] and the gig economy in the United States, there are still strong negative stigmas attached to freelance work. Several of these stigmas are rooted in the (in)stability narrative, based on the precariousness of freelance work and entrepreneurial work in general. Thus, freelancing is sometimes perceived as temporary rather than permanent and valued less than traditional work.

One interviewee discussed this stigma and perception, particularly the perception of freelance work as *unsteady*: 'I think that there is a stigma around it. Because freelancer … It sounds unsteady, right?' Another interviewee expressed similar sentiments that impacted their choice not to use the word *freelancing* when describing their work identity because of the temporary implications it connoted: 'Freelancing just seems like a side gig.'

Because freelancing is a broad occupational term that could apply to very different work across industries, this contributed to a confused understanding of what a freelance work-life looked like. As one interviewee put it, 'I think they think I just sit around.' Another discussed how they had to make an effort to let people know that this was not a job in which they sat around in pyjamas and watched Netflix. These perceptions can lead to fraught relationships with loved ones and hurtful comments. One interviewee talked about parents' perceptions of their occupation: 'Until maybe five years ago, my mom was still suggesting that I try to find a real job.' This idea of the *real job* clearly indicates a more traditional, nine-to-five occupation as an employee at a company, rather than as an independent contractor or small business owner.

Another piece of the (in)stability narrative is the perception that freelance work comes out of necessity because individuals are unable to find

---

[143] L. E. Bridges, 'Flexible as Freedom? The Dynamics of Creative Industry Work and the Case Study of the Editor in Publishing', *New Media & Society*, 20 (2018), 1303–19.

[144] J. Storey, G. Salaman, and K. Platman, 'Living with Enterprise in an Enterprise Economy: Freelance and Contract Workers in the Media', *Human Relations*, 58 (2005), 1033–54.

work or were laid off from previous employment. For the freelancers I interviewed, there was a mix of choice and circumstance involved. Many freelancers purposefully choose to freelance rather than work for an employer in the book industry, but they fight the stigma still. The narrative also persists because it is not completely unfounded; there are plenty of freelancers who are pushed into freelance work because of underemployment or unemployment. Bridges calls the push to freelance work for freelance editors in the book industry a 'pressing concern', and a highly gendered one that marks greater precarity, sporadic work, and fewer opportunities for continuing education in a vulnerable and overcrowded industry. Indeed, in Bridges' own research of freelance editors in the book industry in Australia, she found that the general characteristics and trajectories were thus:

> The editor is more likely to be female, will often start in-house as an unpaid intern or volunteer, learn the craft, make a few vertical steps, and eventually when they have reached the 'glass ceiling' or career potential within one organisation, or, when it comes to child rearing, they will 'opt for' or be 'pushed towards' more flexible work arrangements commonly in the form of freelancing. It has become normalised within the publishing industry, and among editors, to pursue a meaningful career at almost any cost.[145]

While the burden of child-rearing remains mainly on the shoulders of women (and this and other gendered circumstances and structures inhibit and inform occupational identities and trajectories in the book industry), it was also clear from my interviews with freelancers in the book industry in the United States that while some fit the description that Bridges is describing, not all of them did. These freelancers are a heterogeneous group, with many diverse identities, circumstances, and paths to freelance work. Gender and other intersectional aspects will be discussed further in Chapter 3, as they certainly are important contexts for entrepreneurial identity, but I also

---

[145] Bridges, 'Flexible as Freedom', p. 1315.

do not want to overgeneralise by characterising every freelancer in the way that Bridges has.

This stereotype and narrative about the freelance trajectory – particularly for freelance editors – was familiar to the interviewees. One interviewee said, 'I know I have talked to people who've said in the past, especially in journalism, that freelancing meant you couldn't find a job and [it] had stigma to it.' Another interviewee expressed embarrassment about fitting the 'stereotype' of the kind of freelance editor who chose a freelance path in part to align with the circumstances of raising small children.

In the in(stability) narrative and counternarratives, there is another important context to consider. Job turnover and business failures in the traditional book industry are not insignificant. In other words, being employed at a bookstore or a publishing house does not guarantee long-term stability. It is extremely common for book industry professionals to frequently move to different publishing houses, for example. And as disruptive moments like the COVID-19 pandemic have demonstrated, the seemingly 'stable' industry norm can change in an instant. Because of this, one interviewee discussed with me the idea that 'freelancing is the more stable option' in contrast to a 'traditional' job within the book industry. The control afforded to freelancers can be a precarity but also a comfort, especially in times of crisis in the book industry.

2.3 The Busyness Narrative

The perception of Americans as workaholics is a common narrative. A 2019 article in *The Atlantic* called work the new religion of Americans. Labelled 'workism', this religion centres work at the heart of one's identity and purpose in life.[146] Seeing busyness as a 'badge of honor'[147] is deeply ingrained in American culture. Unused vacation time, responding to messages around the clock, and putting in many hours above a normal forty-hour work week are common manifestations of this workaholism for regular employees. For freelancers, the picture gets even more complicated

---

[146] Thompson, *Merchants of Culture*.
[147] M. Wilding, 'The United States of Workaholics', *Medium* (15 March 2018).

because working remotely means that it is technically possible to work at all hours and all the time.

In a study conducted by Reid in 2015, expected professional identities were compared to experienced professional identities. In other words, Reid was analysing how workers navigated and deviated from the 'ideal worker' image:

> People today are expected to be wholly devoted to work, such that they attend to their jobs ahead of all else, including family, personal needs, and even their health. These expectations are personified in the ideal worker image: a definition of the most desirable worker as one who is totally committed to, and always available for, his or her work.[148]

The findings suggest that even when workers do not live up to the 'ideal worker' image, they find ways to portray themselves as conforming to the image.[149] In other words, even when pursuing a better work–life balance, we all want to be perceived as being busy and overworked. Comments such as 'You work too hard' from co-workers or clients are often seen as compliments, with a positive connotation.

Busyness was also a key feature of the narratives from book industry freelancers, either because they were pursuing the ideal worker image or were at least framing themselves as fulfilling that role. One interviewee said, 'I'm too busy right now.' Another described themselves as 'a bit of a workaholic', adding 'Yeah, it's not ideal, but I'm very committed.' In this way, the freelancer frames themselves as being fully committed to the work, in line with the image of the ideal worker.

In justifying working too much, some freelancers evoked the importance of the work to their own identities and self-fulfilment: 'Yeah. I mean, I work

---

[148] E. Reid, 'Embracing, Passing, Revealing, and the Ideal Worker Image: How People Navigate Expected and Experienced Professional Identities', *Organization Science*, 26 (2015), p. 997.

[149] J. Spross, 'Why Workaholics Are Faking Longer Hours – and What That Says about American Businesses', *The Week* (14 May 2015).

all the time. Weekends, you know, all eight-hour-plus days. But I used to have pastimes and then I started putting more time into my business and then that's also my pastime. It's my everything, basically. But I really like it. So it doesn't ever bother me too often.' This statement portrays the kind of career that Americans aspire to have: one that is a calling more than a job, and that passionately consumes all facets of life and energy.

But other freelancers were almost apologetic for working too much, and indicated that the practice was rooted in an inability to draw boundaries, to say no, or to effectively manage their time: 'Yeah, well, I'm not good at it at all. I just work all the time. I worked way too much this year especially. It's hard as a freelancer to turn work down. But I have to get better at it because I just have been taking too much on.' Another freelancer expressed a similar sentiment, tied to the desire not to disappoint others: 'Tricky thing for me is just saying no to projects because I don't want to disappoint any one client too often. And so I tend to say yes, then get myself overscheduled and then that is not good for myself or my family or anything like that.' The financial precarity of freelancing (and entrepreneurship in general) was another factor, and another reason why some freelancers found it hard to turn down work, even when they were overworked: 'I mean, it's hard to say no to projects because if you say yes to projects then that means more money.'

Overwork was the expectation rather than the exception. This was clear in one freelancer's comment about burnout happening to everyone inevitably: 'I mean, everyone gets burned and everyone has to fire a client. Everyone gets fired by a client. You just have to learn from that.' One facet of this expectation was that the overworking would not be eternal, but rather concentrated at the beginning of the freelancing journey and the setting-up of the business, which is why one interview told me 'there's no such thing as work–life balance at first'. But another described this overwork at the beginning as an 'early investment' that was manageable because the freelancer knew they '[weren't] going to do that forever'. In describing the beginning of the freelancing journey, one interviewee talked about how surprised and unprepared they were for how much work it would take:

> There's no way to fully prepare yourself for the fact that you're going to be working two full-time jobs, and I think

it's one of things that doesn't get talked about often. It's very much like how to find the work, how to get the work. And then later you kind of ramp up but not realize this: you're going to be working like seventy-five hours to get paid for forty – get ready. Now, of course, you ramp your rates up to cover that on that nonbillable time. But there's a very small window when you're just starting out, when you're like, what have I done? And that was a surprise. I was unprepared for that.

The ideal worker image can be particularly destructive in terms of the guilt that it imposes upon freelancers who do not feel that they are meeting expectations: 'When you're not working, you feel guilty; that's just the way it's always been.' The constant hum of work disrupted freelancers' efforts to schedule vacation time and set work hours. One freelancer described how they had tried several strategies, with limited success: 'It's difficult, but there's always something that you can and should be doing. There's always emails you're going to be behind on. There's always something that you can be doing. And then, of course, you know, online you see other editors trying things and thinking, maybe I should be doing that, too.'

To justify the position of the freelancer in the book industry, there also emerged a sub-narrative not only of busyness, but of this busyness being proof of freelancers being extra disciplined – more so than other types of workers or entrepreneurs: 'It takes a certain kind of discipline to work from home. I learned that really fast. You can't go down to see what's in the fridge every twenty minutes.' Confronted with the flexibility of working from home and setting your own schedule, freelancing is portrayed as something that requires extra discipline to work hard within an environment that could be conducive to less work, or at least a better work–life balance.

2.4 The Freedom Narrative

Freedom, primarily in the form of flexibility, was repeatedly narrated as the primary benefit of freelancing. This is the compromise: for all the instability and busyness, the flexibility makes freelancing worth it.[150] The freedom rhetoric centres individual freedom for freelancers 'to work where and when they want'. Mathisen[151] found that freedom and autonomy were two key motivations for freelancers in the field of journalism. Similarly, in examining the discourse of freelance journalists, Edstrom and Ladendorf found that the word *freedom* was a nodal point in the discourse: 'In the narratives, this included freedom from oppressive aspects of work as an employee such as bosses, disgruntled co-workers, unrewarding work tasks, etc.'[152] Especially in contrast to the negative narratives about insecurities related to freelance work, Edstrom and Ladendorf found that their interviewees celebrated the flexible advantages of freelance work:[153]

> In the narratives of the freelancers, the aspect of freedom that seemed the most important, and was also judged as the most positive, was the freelancers' power to decide over how they used their own time. Even though some of them started to freelance for other reasons (often they had been more pushed than pulled into self-employment), most of them said they would find it hard to go back to work in organizations.[154]

In the interviews, the freedom to be flexible is juxtaposed with the additional need to be disciplined to be productive: 'One of the best things about being a freelancer is the flexibility. But you also need the structure to make sure you're being productive.' Sometimes it was specifically for the flexibility that an individual made the switch; as one interviewee recalled: 'I'd been thinking about freelancing for a while before that because I wanted the flexibility.' One of the main flexibility threads was flexibility in terms of

---

[150] Bridges, 'Flexible as Freedom', p. 1305.

[151] Mathisen, 'Entrepreneurs and Idealists'.

[152] M. Edstrom and M. Ladendorf, 'Freelance Journalists as a Flexible Workforce in Media Industries', *Journalism Practice*, 6 (2012), p. 716.

[153] Edstrom and Ladendorf, 'Freelance Journalists as a Flexible Workforce', p. 712.

[154] Edstrom and Ladendorf, 'Freelance Journalists as a Flexible Workforce', p. 717.

time: freelancers can work during the times and days that they want. One interviewee suggested that flexibility was conducive to producing the best work: 'Freedom allows you to do the best work possible. You can do it when it's best for you, not based on when someone else is determined it's the best time to be there.' Additionally, this flexibility of time could contribute to a better work–life balance and overall career satisfaction: 'You want a work–life balance. So you might work just as many hours, but you can structure your family life around your business rather than the business driving your family life.'

However, there are other ways, beyond time, in which the interviewees expressed both flexibility and freedom – for example, the freedom to choose the kinds of clients and projects that they'd prefer: 'The freedom to pursue those instead of having to ask someone else for permission makes your workday easier.' There is the lifestyle flexibility that is afforded when you do not have to go into an office, especially for parents raising children: 'I had a few kids along the way, so during that time that was handy to have the flexibility of freelancing.' There is also the freedom of being one's own boss: 'I realise it would take a crap tonne of money to make me give up my business just because I love it. I love being my own boss.' One interviewee referred to this freedom to be one's own boss as 'calling the shots'. Another interviewee discussed the extra tasks that would fall upon her shoulders as a woman in a traditional office environment, but as her own boss that was no longer the case:

> But having that freedom is amazing. I've worked in a few office environments and especially as a woman, some- times you kind of get handed those extra tasks, you know, take notes at a meeting and you'll do the follow- up. And all those little things don't happen when you're working in this situation. So there's that extra freedom that you're just responsible for yourself and obviously your clients.

A final node of the freedom discourse was centred around geographical freedom. As the interviewed freelancers came from all over the United

States, their geographical locations were usually determined by factors other than their work: coming back to the place where they grew up, moving for a partner's job, moving somewhere more rural for work–life balance, staying in a location where they were working in a traditional job in addition to freelancing, etc. Of the 'ability to move around', one interviewee said this:

> If you're a freelancer, you're unattached. If you want to be a digital nomad, that's a thing you can do theoretically with freelance work. Or if you're like me and you have a partner that has some flexibility, it just opens up a lot of different options that do not exist for the people I know that have really bought into the corporate ladder.

Of course, 'unattached' is an interesting term in this narrative, because while it comes with advantages such as geographic flexibility, being unattached also connotes being less socially connected to other professionals in the field, which can be particularly difficult for freelancers.

Despite these key elements in the narratives of freedom from freelancers in the book industry, it is worth noting that there are still many ways in which freelancers are not 'free'. Freelancers in the book industry are not always able to set their own rates. When working directly with publishers, they are tied to the rates that the publisher sets, which are much lower than book industry freelancers can charge when working with others such as academics, individual authors, and companies outside of the book industry. Due to this situation, some of the interviewees discussed with me the choice to work less with publishers and more with these other groups or individuals. However, for other interviewees, the prestige and symbolic capital that came with working with publishers (particularly the Big Five) was too valuable to give up, even when the hourly or project rate was lower. Similarly, the 'freedom' of flexible time is a double-edged sword in that being able to work whenever and wherever also means that freelancers can be working all the time, and that work–life balance quickly becomes more of a fantasy than a reality. Interestingly, Bridges found in her research that the 'flexible as freedom' narrative was more common among female freelancers in the book industry, whereas male freelancers experienced greater unease with the insecurity that this flexibility and freedom provided.[155] There certainly is a gender disparity associated with the freedom narrative. Bridges found that women could tolerate precarity better than men in the freelance book editing sphere,[156] which may be connected to the common scenario in which a female freelancer is able to rely on a partner's income or benefits (such as health insurance) as a 'fall back' in order to mitigate risk.

Freelancers in the book industry respond to the discourse of many other general narratives about freelancing in their own narratives about their occupational identities and experiences. The stereotypes about the temporary, unstable, and less desirable nature of freelance work requires additional work from book industry freelancers to justify via narratives their choices and circumstances as freelancers. Likewise, cultural narratives and discourse in the United States around occupational identities and lifestyles emphasise workism as almost a religion, and busyness as a badge of honour. Thus, freelancers in the book industry either conform to extreme patterns of busyness, portray themselves as conforming to these patterns to fit the 'ideal worker' and 'ideal entrepreneur' image, or express guilt or apologise for the ways that they align with or work against this narrative. Yet the freedom narrative was perhaps the narrative most at the core of book industry freelancing, manifest in terms of control over tasks and clients, freedom from gendered and restrictive traditional work conditions, geographical flexibility, flexibility of time, etc. The narrative spins this freedom as almost unfettered, even though it is clear that there are constraints in freelancing too, ways in which freelancers are not free, and maybe less free than traditional workers or other entrepreneurs. Still, these three narratives represent the key components of occupational identity, as expressed through narrative, for freelancers in the book industry.

---

[155] Bridges, 'Flexible as Freedom', p. 1310.
[156] Bridges, 'Flexible as Freedom', p. 1315.

3 Intersectionality and Entrepreneurial Identity

In the introduction to this book I established core characteristics of identities: identities are positions within social groups, individuals can have multiple identities, identities are complex, identities are fluid, identities are situational, identities require work to maintain, and identities are produced in dialogue and narrative. These characteristics were established primarily to discuss entrepreneurial identity – a kind of occupational identity. But because identities are multiple and complex, it would be neglectful to consider entrepreneurial identity in isolation and not examine how entrepreneurial identity intersects with other identities that an individual holds. For that reason, this chapter will focus on one more characteristic of identities: identities are intersectional.

Intersectionality is a term introduced by Kimberlé Crenshaw in 1989 in her foundational work on the marginalization of Black women in law, theory, and politics.[157] Crenshaw used intersectionality to expose narratives that maintained existing power relations and elevate narratives of resistance from marginalised groups that came in response to those power structures. Intersectionality is defined as a 'method and a disposition, a heuristic and analytic tool'.[158] In their mapping of the movements of the theory of intersectionality, Carbado et al. encouraged all scholars to 'endeavor, on an ongoing basis, to move intersectionality to unexplored places'.[159] Certainly, entrepreneurship is one of those places for which more exploration is necessary in terms of intersectionality.

That's not to say that intersectionality has been entirely neglected in entrepreneurial identity research. In Watson's 2009 case study, he found that personal and family lives as well as individual identities were 'closely

---

[157] K. Crenshaw, 'Demarginalizing the Intersection of Race and Sex: A Black Feminist Critique of Antidiscrimination Doctrine, Feminist Theory and Antiracist Politics'. *University of Chicago Legal Forum*, 139 (1989). https://chicagounbound.uchicago.edu/uclf/vol1989/iss1/8.

[158] D. W. Carbado, K. W. Crenshaw, V. M. Mays, and B. Tomlinson, 'Intersectionality: Mapping the Movements of a Theory', *Du Bois Review: Social Science Research on Race*, 10 (2013), p. 312.

[159] Carbado, Crenshaw, Mays, and Tomlinson, 'Intersectionality: Mapping the Movements of a Theory', p. 305.

intertwined with the strategic shaping of the enterprises in which they [entrepreneurs] are involved'.[160] Larson and Pearson, in their research on the role of place in entrepreneurial identity, noted how this entrepreneurial identity intersected other aspects of identity: 'Occupations or professions serve as key markers of social identity, help individuals narrate a sense of self, and provide a way for managing and organizing other aspects of identity such as gender, race, and class.'[161] Indeed, Essers and Benschop studied the intersectionality of entrepreneurs who were female, living in the Netherlands, and of Moroccan or Turkish origin.[162] Phillips et al. found in their case studies that entrepreneurs utilised other aspects of their identities to make meaningful connections that helped their businesses. From their data, they found common narratives to construct ties surrounding 'shared religious identity, shared nationality, shared experience of migration, and a sense of shared trauma'.[163]

Based on the most recent Survey of Business Owners gathered from the United States Census Bureau, 32 per cent of small businesses in the United States are owned by women and 26 per cent by racial minorities.[164] Data about the demographics of the book industry in the United States has been primarily focused on publishers and literary agents. Data on the demographics for booksellers, distributors, freelancers, and authors remains more elusive. If we look at publishers and literary agents, then the 2019 snapshot of the industry shows that it is 76 per cent white, 74 per cent cis women, 81 per cent straight, and 89 per cent non-disabled. But this is a broad-stroke picture of identity in the industry, and in terms of entrepreneurial identity this book is more concerned with the idiosyncratic, individual accounts of entrepreneurs within their specific intersectional identities.[165]

---

[160] Watson, 'Entrepreneurial Action', p. 265.

[161] Larson and Pearson, 'Placing Identity', p. 243.

[162] Essers and Benschop, 'Enterprising Identities'.

[163] Phillips, Tracey, and Karra, 'Building Entrepreneurial Tie Portfolios', p. 135.

[164] US Census Bureau, 'Survey of Business Owners (SBO): Survey Results: 2012'. www.census.gov/library/publications/2012/econ/2012-sbo.html

[165] Leeandlowbooks, 'Where Is the Diversity in Publishing? The 2019 Diversity Baseline Survey Results', Lee & Low Books: The Open Book Blog (28 January 2020).

While cis women are the largest category, at least of publishers and literary agents, there are still many gendered structures and biases (even towards cis women) in book industry entrepreneurship. In the academic space, women are often ignored in entrepreneurship research or viewed as failing due to certain measurements of performance and success.[166]

Many of the narratives surrounding entrepreneurship not only tend to be gendered, but more specifically tend to be gendered cis male. The narrative of the entrepreneur as a classic hero, as the 'self-made man', and others all presume that entrepreneurship is a male endeavour. As Hamilton noted, 'An assumption that entrepreneurship is a masculine endeavour, and that entrepreneurial identity is most naturally male, stubbornly endures in entrepreneurship research. It replicates and reinforces what seems at times surprising gender blindness in the field.'[167] The gendered nature of entrepreneurship and entrepreneurship narratives also permeates management and organizational identity spaces in the business world. One interviewee commented, 'It feels different to be a woman running a business than a man. And we have interacted with male entrepreneurs and it has a very different kind of culture around it.' While this female interviewee was unable to put her finger on exactly what that cultural difference was, she recognised that

---

[166] Hamilton, 'Whose Story Is It Anyway?'; Hamilton, 'Entrepreneurial Narrative Identity and Gender'; Duberley and Carrigan, 'The Career Identities of "Mumpreneurs"'; A. Colli, P. F. Pérez, and M. B. Rose, 'National Determinants of Family Firm Development? Family Firms in Britain, Spain, and Italy in the Nineteenth and Twentieth Centuries', *Enterprise & Society*, 4 (2003) 28–64; S. Baines and J. Wheelock, J. 'Working for Each Other: Gender, the Household and Micro-Business Survival and Growth', *International Small Business Journal*, 17 (1998), 16–35; K. Mulholland, 'Gender Power and Property Relations within Entrepreneurial Wealthy Families', *Gender, Work & Organization*, 3 (1996), 78–102; K. Mirchandani, 'Feminist Insight on Gendered Work: New Directions in Research on Women and Entrepreneurship', *Gender, Work & Organization*, 6 (1999), 224–35; A. Bruni, S. Gherardi, and B. Poggio, *Gender and Entrepreneurship: An Ethnographic Approach* (Abingdon: Routledge, 2004).

[167] Hamilton, 'Entrepreneurial Narrative Identity and Gender', p. 705.

she did things differently to male entrepreneurs and that she was perceived differently to how male entrepreneurs were perceived.

Though cis white women are plentiful in the publishing industry, they often occupy undervalued and supporting roles. As one interviewee noted: 'There were women in the industry, but they were more in junior positions. So there's still a lot of that.' Similarly, a female interviewee who had a partner with an income and benefits expressed frustration about what this situation looked like from the outside: 'My income is the second income, which I find horribly frustrating, infuriating, as a huge undervaluing of what is largely women's work.' While there certainly is an economic privilege that comes with having a partner's income or health insurance to rely on, one interviewee noted how this privilege allowed her to navigate and break the boundaries of certain gender privileges. Her business approach was much less aggressive and more collaborative – both characteristics that have been identified as a more feminist approach but less highly valued in the business world – and she discussed how the financial backing of her partner's income allowed her to run her business the way that she wanted to, and the way that felt authentic to her.

The independent narrative, in addition to portraying smallness, economic dependence, and a locally rooted and diversity-focused philosophy, also has a component of being less gendered, or at least more friendly, to entrepreneurs outside of the cis white male identity. One interviewee put it this way: 'We're aware that in the big houses, it's male dominated. But in our little corner of the world, it's all women. I mean, men tend to be the CEO' – but, this interviewee argues, that is not the case in the independent space.

Sometimes cis male clients or colleagues treat women, non-binary, or trans book industry entrepreneurs poorly. One freelancer noted: 'There are still sometimes clients, especially from more male-centred cultures that will kind of talk down to me or to the other women and I'll have to step in and really assert myself. And I imagine that that would be even harder if I were transgender or non-binary.' Another freelancer recounted, 'But I think I've had a couple clients where if I had been male, the experience would have been different and the experience would have been better.' This same interviewee discussed how her feminine voice impacted a male client's refusal to take her advice and how advice given to a female client about a sensitivity reader was ignored due to the perception that the editor was 'overly sensitive'. Because of negative past experiences with men in the industry, one interviewee said, 'I felt a lot more comfortable working with women. They just seemed to be nicer.'

One interviewee discussed white males trying to take away her power:

> One of the most uncomfortable experiences I had was as a guest at a local writing programme. I talked about publishing and community and why we all have to work together. A white male student raised his hand and said, 'You're not giving me any hope. I thought you were going to tell me how I was going to get my book published. And you're not even helping me at all. You're not telling me how to get my book published.' I had been talking for an hour. I had told them how to do research for the market. In that moment, it was such a direct attack; it was just in a very aggressive, very negative way. It's like he was very pointedly saying, 'Who are you to be knowledgeable?' But one by one, the women in the room took the question and berated him for his expectations of what I could bring. They said, 'You need to apologise to her for how you said this or how you are treating her. She is a guest in our programme. She is a guest in our home. Everything she told you is right. There is no easy way to get published and you shouldn't take it out on her.'

This interviewee expressed the frustration of taking the time to share knowledge and give back to the community only to have her authority and legitimacy questioned by men such as this male student.

One woman used only her first initial rather than her full first name in sending emails because she 'was concerned about the sexism that is inherent in people'. In response, the overwhelming majority of emails said 'Mr. X is very qualified'. Most people assumed she was male. If she replied using her full first name,

offers would tend to disappear. Things would not follow
through. When I was a woman and when they thought I was
a man, then I was more qualified. They offered me more
money and they were more interested to work with me.
When they knew I was a woman, I got told I was doing
pretty good, but can do some training.

While parents (especially mothers) emphasised the advantage of the
flexibility of entrepreneurial work in balancing parenthood and business,
some also felt that their parenthood made their business less legitimate:
working from home is not just for moms. The shame and guilt associated
with contributing to a 'stereotype' was evident from mothers as well: 'I was
a mom and I started part time as a little side gig without specific training.
I certainly feel like I'm some sort of stereotype.' Another said, 'Sometimes
I have been pigeonholed as having a mommy job.'

One childless interviewee talked about the difficulty of working in the
children's book industry, where freelance clients expected her to have
children: 'I certainly get clients who wonder at the fact that I don't have
kids. So with those ones, I have to tell them I work with kids all the time.
Volunteer and work at a bookstore. It's like having children is like market
research and if you don't have children, how can you really understand
children's books?' One has to wonder, would those same clients be asking
the same questions if the freelancer were a cis man?

For some book industry entrepreneurs, racial identity and lived racial
experience are the catalysts for entrepreneurial work. A bookseller talked
about being 'mixed Puerto Rican and Indigenous American'. With this
identity, she had a mother who 'always worked really hard to have quality
books so I didn't grow up with this idea that I didn't exist in literature'. Her
mother was a librarian by profession, and this bookseller spent her childhood in
libraries and with books where she could see people like her in the pages. One
of the catalysts for starting her own bookshop was to give other children that
same opportunity to see themselves in books, which is why the shop advocates
for diverse children's books, including those with BIPOC characters.

A Black woman publisher likewise described racial identity and experience as fuelling entrepreneurial desire. She said, 'As a kid, I didn't see any

books that were written by Black doctors, cookbooks, or any other type of book. And so for little girls or for boys, I want them to see.' Driven by a passion to help children see themselves in books, this interviewee founded her own publishing company.

Racial diversity – or, more importantly, the lack thereof – is not a new topic of conversation in the book industry, but it illustrates the glacial pace at which the industry changes. BIPOC book industry professionals, authors, and characters are still grossly underrepresented, even in YA and children's books where the movement has had the most momentum.[168] Being a white book industry professional and entrepreneur is a privileged space, as one interviewee notes:

> I think being a white person makes it easier. People's response when you tell them that you're a freelancer, for example. I suspect that being a white person saying that I'm out on my own, I get a little bit more positive response. And people of colour are perceived as doing a thing that was necessary, where I'm making a choice.

This interviewee brings up a very interesting question: first, is it assumed that white people choose entrepreneurship (especially freelance entrepreneurship), but BIPOC individuals pursue entrepreneurship out of necessity? If this assumption does exist, it is certainly tied to the perception that entrepreneurship is perceived more favourably, and spun in more favourable narratives, if it is viewed as a choice rather than a necessity borne of underemployment or unemployment.

Religion as an aspect of identity was not discussed by many of the interviewees, but it did come up. Here, it was clear that there were intersectional differences with religious and racial identities as well. Three interviewees talked about the importance of their Christian faiths in shaping their identities and entrepreneurship, and two of those interviewees were

---

[168] J. Kimura, 'A Cover is Worth 1000 Words: Visibility and Racial Diversity in Young Adult Cover Design'. *PDX Scholar* (2019). https://pdxscholar.library .pdx.edu/cgi/viewcontent.cgi?article=1035&context=eng_bookpubpaper

Black women. One woman talked about her relationship with God and praying about business matters to make sure that she was headed down the right path. Another viewed her religion as essential to her personal integrity: 'In terms of faith, I see it as being essential. In terms of the integrity that I have to have. And in terms of wanting to manage the standards that I go to the market with.' All three of these interviewees also had close business ties with the Christian publishing and bookselling community.

Religion was also an important context for shaping an individual's early life, even when that person had moved away from religion in the end. One interviewee discussed how an upbringing in the Church of Jesus Christ of Latter-Day Saints (commonly called the Mormon Church) shaped her early perception of gender roles and stunted her entrepreneurship and career in specific ways. Another interviewee chose to work primarily with women after growing up in an evangelical family where 'we were taught the man is the head of the household, must do everything that he says'. Again, the rigid gender roles that came from that structure formed a resolve within this interviewee to run her business a certain way.

Both gender and race influence the opportunities an individual has as an entrepreneur, the gates that are open to them, biased treatment from others in the industry because of their gender and/or racial identities, and the reasons why a person may choose to pursue entrepreneurship in the first place. Gender and race were two large categories that were discussed by many of the interviewees, but there were other identities that came up as well, and that impacted entrepreneurial identity.

One interviewee discussed publishing entrepreneurship as being well suited to autism: taking calculated risks, solving problems, and being given autonomy and independence to solve the problem that you were sent to solve. In fact, this interviewee attributed the success of the publishing company to the unique way that he thought and made decisions due to his neurodivergence. Another interviewee discussed her neurodivergence as well, but she was much less open and public about that identity:

> I haven't spoken publicly about my brain injury or my neurodivergence, but I'm definitely neurodivergent. I haven't used that as my publishing identity, but I've

thought about it more because there are things like this because of how my brain works these days and I become more comfortable with my identity as someone who is different, who thinks differently. And that would create a whole other set of suspicions, I think. But also there would be something really empowering about having that be part of our press identity. And my public identity is very vulnerable. I haven't ever put it on social media. I never talk about it.

This striking comment prompts the question that each individual entrepreneur must grapple with: How much should my personal identity be part of my business brand? This can be especially hard for micro-enterprises, with very few (if any) employees, and where the personality and brand of the owner/manager/entrepreneur can become the default brand of the overall business. In terms of the two interviewees who discussed their neurodivergence, for one it was an important part of identity and brand for both the individual and the business, but for the other their neurodivergence identity impacted their entrepreneurial behaviour but was deemed too personal and vulnerable to put out into the world in such a public way.

There were two interviewees who talked about sexual identity in a similar way: it was a personal identity that shaped them, but they were wary of sharing it with others or portraying it as part of a business brand. One interviewee said, 'I also identify as bisexual. And it's not something that I write about a lot, but it is something that at times I wonder like how much, you know, to include something like that in my writing and how much to lean into, like should I write it for LGBT publications?' Another interviewee said, 'I don't consider myself 100 per cent straight and I'm not ashamed of that. I also think that it opens a can of worms with being a business owner that I don't feel like it's anybody's business.' Only one interviewee talked very openly about not being straight, specifically as regards representation of lesbians in the places she had lived and in literature: 'Those lesbians have their own little boxes, so I was in this little box. In certain cities, it's like only gay men exist. Gay women don't exist.' Here, the interviewee highlights being part of the broader queer community, but also feeling isolated from it when she sees the representation of that community being limited only to gay men. The intersection of her gender identity as a woman and her queer identity makes a big difference in terms of belonging and representation.

Differing abilities and illnesses were also identities held by some of the interviewees. One interviewee had chronic pain and fibromyalgia. This impacted their scheduling and capacity to keep the business running:

> This year has been a little tough because I have fibromyalgia, and all this year has been a fibromyalgia flare, so I'm exhausted and I'm also running my business. So that's been really challenging. Today I feel like falling asleep right now. So that's been the unfortunate part where if I had a traditional job, I would have sick time and get paid if I had to take a day off.

Here, this interviewee portrays one of the negative factors of being an entrepreneur, which is that there is no paid sick time off – something that might be available if working for an employer. On the other hand, there can be benefits of entrepreneurship and the entrepreneur lifestyle for coping with differing abilities and illness. For example, one interviewee talked about dealing with multiple sclerosis: 'I like my job fit super well. There are a lot of limitations that I have. So the job is awesome.' The flexibility and control offered by entrepreneurship helped this individual to manage the limitations of MS.

Even in terms of something as simple as location, an intersectional identity approach demonstrates the power structures and hierarchies that open opportunities for some and close them for others. Chapter 1 discussed the intersection and impact of place on entrepreneurial identity. Larson and Pearson's study of entrepreneurs in Montana found that place and entrepreneurship intersected interview discourse through place as lifestyle, place as home, and place as challenge narratives. But some of the most important findings from Larson and Pearson's study relate to how place impacts intersectional identities. The Montana entrepreneurs use place in a way to frame particular gendered, raced, and classed occupational identities. For instance, by describing his decision to locate his business in Montana and to participate in the recreational activities such a locale provides, an entrepreneur portrays and constructs a middle-class, White, masculine identity. Such a portrayal has socially desirable connotations that would be politically incorrect to frame in more direct ways. In a sense, place may be a more socially acceptable discursive means in today's world to embrace and perpetuate masculinity and whiteness.[169]

Using place to frame gendered, raced, and classed occupational identities is, of course, not unique to entrepreneurs in Montana. To use Portland, Oregon, as an example, since that is where I live and direct a graduate programme in book publishing, the situation is very similar. Portland is known for its recreational activities such as kayaking, hiking, camping, rowing, etc., and these leisurely outdoor activities are costly and primarily available to middle-class, white men. Portland also presents a brand narrative encompassed in 'keep Portland weird' that embraces diversity. But despite its left-leaning politics, Portland is one of the whitest places in the United States, and the 'weirdness' it embraces only extends within the sphere of 'diversity' that the community finds comfortable. This relates to Larson and Pearson's findings that the identity narratives of Montana apply to specific types of entrepreneurs, which means they might be unappealing or unavailable to other entrepreneurs:

> This identification may serve to segregate people to certain places according to gender, race, and class. For entrepreneurs who can narrate themselves into the larger narrative of Missoula, Montana, there may be no better place. As a result, we find White, male entrepreneurs choosing to (re)locate in Missoula. Those of other classes, races, and genders may not find these narratives of place as appealing, however, as it

---

[169] Larson and Pearson, 'Placing Identity', p. 261.

may be difficult to locate oneself in a narrative that has been historically and materially unavailable. In an increasingly diverse America, this possibility has profound implications for relatively homogeneous locales such as Missoula and efforts of community leaders to bring in more high-tech entrepreneurs as the identity narrative afforded by Missoula appeals to an increasingly narrow segment of society. This exclusivity makes the identity more attractive to some but is problematic in the sense that it may also contribute to the material segregation of bodies according to race and gender.[170]

While Larson and Pearson focus specifically on race, gender, and class, there are many other identities that one might consider in this same argument (such as [dis]ability, religion, neurodivergence, and sexuality). Entrepreneurship in publishing – regardless of location – can be either a very privileged or a little-privileged space. It is highly polar in this way.

In summary, there were various identities that came out of the interviews with book industry entrepreneurs, and these identities intersected with and impacted entrepreneurship and entrepreneurial identity. This intersection influenced the way that other people (including clients, readers, etc.) treated entrepreneurs. It also impacted how the entrepreneur was perceived – sometimes as less knowledgeable or less qualified based on their perceived identity. In other words, intersecting identities created an environment that made some entrepreneurs uncomfortable in certain places or situations or led to greater imposter syndrome. Intersecting identities were also key to the reasons why entrepreneurs decided to pursue entrepreneurship and the unique way that those entrepreneurs solved problems.

[170] Larson and Pearson, 'Placing Identity', p. 262.

Conclusion and COVID-19

Entrepreneurs in the book industry are a group of heterogenous individuals who are shaped by the contexts in which their entrepreneurship is situated. The theme that unites them all is entrepreneurial identity and the various ways that they portray and build that identity through narratives. The research question that this book has addressed is this: How do entrepreneurs in the US book industry utilise narratives to frame and construct entrepreneurial identity? In the book industry, we see entrepreneurial narratives of independence, culture over commerce, accidental profession, place, risk, (in)stability, busyness, and freedom. All of these narratives are constructed and performed within larger cultural narratives, such as the American Dream and the positive portrayal of entrepreneurship in US culture.

Entrepreneurship in the book industry is filled with polarizations and contradictions. Entrepreneurs themselves are part of a polarization in the industry: small businesses, as contrasted with megacorporations.[171] But book industry entrepreneurs are also polarised in terms of privilege. In some ways, entrepreneurship is a very privileged space within the book industry. Often entrepreneurs pursue this path for cultural rather than economic reward and rely on financial support from partners or family. Additionally, racially the book industry is a predominantly white space, which means that many entrepreneurs in that space benefit from white privilege. On the other hand, entrepreneurship is a space of little privilege, one wherein someone who faces barriers to employment or safe working environments can take control in an industry with low start-up costs and create something new. The complexity is such that entrepreneurs hold privilege in some ways and lack it in others, as with white cis women who face gendered institutions and bias, but who benefit from white privilege and often economic privilege if they have a partner who is traditionally employed. All book industry entrepreneurs lack privilege in respect of some of the risks they are forced to take, including in supplying (or foregoing) their own healthcare. They might be privileged by access to

[171] A. D. Brown, 'A Narrative Approach to Collective Identities', *Journal of Management Studies*, 43 (2006), 731–53.

greater fulfilment, passion, and flexibility, yet lack privilege because they did not fit or were pushed out of traditional employment spaces. Entrepreneurship in the book industry could be perceived as a means of empowerment whereby entrepreneurs can take back control and power, or as a form of bondage for those who are forced into entrepreneurship when they feel they have no other choice.

While this book has not been able to capture all entrepreneurs in the book industry, the groups that it has addressed (primarily booksellers, publishers, and freelancers) identify entrepreneurialism on a spectrum. As was addressed in Chapter 2, for example, freelancers have various approaches to their practices, some more business-oriented and entrepreneurially oriented than others, including hiring of employees or business incorporation. Publishers and booksellers exist on a spectrum of entrepreneurial identity too. We might also consider this spectrum for things like risk, location, and innovation for the three groups (booksellers, publishers, and freelancers). For example, the financial risk for production in the book industry lies with the publisher, as does the risk for inventory of returns from bookshops. But bookshops take the risk for the physical space, and authors take the risk for the labour required to produce the book. Of all three, the bookseller has the most risk in terms of start-up costs because of the requisite physical space and over-heads, but there are many ways in which the publisher takes greater risks overall. In terms of location, even though all three types of entrepreneurs in the book industry position location in their narratives, location is most important to the narratives of booksellers and least important to the narratives of freelancers. A spectrum perspective helps to illustrate the heterogeneity of the different entrepreneurial groups and the ways in which entrepreneurial identity shifts within those categories as well.

To conclude this analysis of twenty-first-century entrepreneurship in the book industry in the United States, it seems appropriate to tie things up by looking at a specific context: COVID-19. Entrepreneurship is defined by the ability to cope with risk and uncertainty, particularly in times of disruption.[172] What better case study to illustrate entrepreneurial identity,

---

[172] Koudstaal, Sloof, and Van Praag, 'Risk, Uncertainty, and Entrepreneurship, pp. 2897–915.

narratives, and behaviour in the twenty-first-century book industry than through the disruption caused by the global pandemic. In many ways, COVID-19 was a catalyst for entrepreneurial thinking. While entrepreneurs experience many personal disruptions within their own professional journeys and identities, the difference with COVID-19 was that the pandemic disrupted the whole industry, and life more generally, for everyone, meaning that the entire book industry was pushed into an entrepreneurial state and mentality. As one entrepreneur aptly stated, 'Adaptation is an essential characteristic of life and survival'. Another put it this way: 'We've had to think in that entrepreneurial way again, like what are the things we can do?'

COVID-19 provided some conflict to the busyness narrative, not only for freelancers but for publishers and booksellers as well. One bookseller noted,

> During the shutdown it was actually kind of nice that I was just in the shop, Monday through Friday, and then I was home on the weekends and every evening; that was really fun. To kind of have that regular job experience again. And it makes me kind of not want to go back to doing the Friday and Saturday nights and realize, well, you know, maybe I don't need to have all those buying hours, maybe we can find other people to work those evening shifts, so that I can be home more often.

Others still maintained the narrative of busyness, saying things like 'things got much busier here', 'I am busier than ever before', and 'business is going better than ever'. This was particularly to counter the idea that business would be slower during the pandemic, which it was for some entrepreneurs, but not for others. Especially at the beginning of the COVID-19 shutdown (around end of March and early April), the narratives in the media were focused on mindfulness, self-care, pursuing hobbies, and not focusing so much on productivity. As part of these larger narratives, some entrepreneurs found that their own narratives of work–life balance and hobby time were changing too:

> Until COVID, the entire year before, I did not do anything
> with hobbies. All hobby time went to my business. I decided
> I would take 'me time' and do my hobby: making collages.
> I love it. I have been doing that on weekends. Now I'm
> realizing to keep up with everything I am going to have to
> go back to no hobby time.

While the pandemic disruption did not create a better work–life balance for everyone, it was a disruption that required entrepreneurs to creatively reposition, renarrate, and rethink their processes, purposes, and structures.

Entrepreneurs, one could argue, are better prepared than most individuals to deal with disruption and change, since they willingly pursue it occupationally. This was expressed by the book industry entrepreneurs who saw the flexibility of entrepreneurship as a benefit that allowed them to be more agile, especially since many of them had already been working from home (particularly publishers and freelancers): '[B]ecause I was already working from home and communicating with the bulk of my network remotely, quarantine hasn't been the challenge for me that it's been for a lot of people.' Another interviewee said, 'Freelancing has let me be nimble to economic shifts that might have had a greater impact if I relied on a single employer.'

But book industry entrepreneurs were not unaffected by the disruption of the pandemic, particularly along gendered and racial lines. Some of the increased busyness was the product of what one interviewee called 'the staggeringly ridiculous number of teacher/admin emails and Zoom meetings for my son's online distance learning'. While certainly all parents experienced the disruption of having children and their workspace now in the same proximity, mothers bore the brunt of this burden: 'I definitely feel the impact in terms of the pandemic's effect on gender roles that has been recognised in media reports.' Childcare was described in terms of 'juggling', and sometimes as 'a nightmare'. One mother lamented:

> We still have our babysitter two and a half days per week
> and we have established a so-called 'social bubble' with her,
> but now half the week I'm working while also taking care of

very busy five-year-old twins. It sounds as if school is not
going to be full time, so this is going to go on for a while.
I really miss my previous schedule.

On top of the implications for occupational identity and work productivity, some entrepreneurs had to grapple with what message this gendered
divide gave to the children they were raising:

> I'm trying to take the long view and hope that I'll be able to
> refocus on my career progression more deeply in five or ten
> years, when the kids are grown and out of the house. I feel
> torn because it's definitely the right thing to do given the
> circumstances and there's no other good answer right now,
> but I regret the long-term impact that it's likely to have,
> both on my career and on how my children grow up viewing
> work and gender.

On top of the pandemic, which already disproportionately impacted
Black people in the United States,[173] George Floyd was brutally murdered
by police in Minnesota in May 2020. This was a catalyst for Black Lives
Matter protests across the United States. One interviewee lived in downtown Minneapolis near where protests were happening and had to evacuate
to live with a spouse's parents for five nights. Sirens and helicopters
throughout the day impacted her ability to focus and concentrate. Other
individuals took part in protests themselves, and generally felt the heavy
weight and anxiety of the matter.

Mental health, depression, stress, and anxiety were all topics that arose
surrounding occupational identity around the pandemic. One interviewee
described this feeling as 'mushy brain': 'There are some days things are not
clicking and it feels impossible to developmental edit.' The constantly
changing information and nature of the pandemic and other national

---

[173] National Urban League, *State of Black America: Unmasked* (2020): http://
sobadev.iamempowered.com/sites/soba.iamempowered.com/files/NUL-
SOBA-2020-ES-web.pdf.

phenomena (such as Black Lives Matter movements) impacted individual mental health and work schedules: 'When we got the stay-at-home orders, I was so anxious that I could not concentrate. So I ended up being a week late on a project.'

The impact of the disruption caused by the pandemic has not been uniform. Much like entrepreneurial identities and opportunities, context is key: 'I'm fortunate that the pandemic hasn't affected me substantially, especially in comparison with low-income people, essential workers, minority communities, etc. Everything I'll say below is to be taken in that context – that is, I recognise how fortunate I am in life overall, and I don't take that for granted. Everything is minor in comparison.' Even the hopeful attitude that characterises entrepreneurial personality in so much of the literature[174] might be said to be a privileged position. One interviewee reflected on her initial response to the pandemic: 'I just had to trust that everything was going to work out because it always had before. Then I said that to a friend and realised how white privilege it was. Everything has always worked out for me. And I realised what a white privilege statement that was.'

The accounts from these book entrepreneurs in response to the COVID-19 pandemic demonstrate the contradictions in narratives, the ways that entrepreneurial narratives change to accommodate fluid occupational identities, and the intersectional narratives that emerge. Even in times of massive disruption, these narratives shape entrepreneurial identity as core to an individual self: 'Publishing has always been my meaning and purpose as a marginalized person that gets me out of bed every morning, but in moments of crisis it also serves that purpose for the world at large – to share skills and frame an issue in a way that they suddenly find themselves interested in.'

[174] H. Brandstätter, 'Personality Aspects of Entrepreneurship: A Look at Five Meta-Analyses. Personality and Individual Differences', *Personality and Individual Differences*, 51 (2011), 222–30.

Bibliography

Agrawal, A., Catalini, C., Goldfarb, A., and Luo, H. (2018). 'Slack Time and Innovation'. *Organization Science*, 29(6), 1056–73.

Ahl, H. (2006). 'Why Research on Women Entrepreneurs Needs New Directions'. *Entrepreneurship Theory and Practice*, 30(5), 595–621.

Ainsworth, S., and Hardy, C. (2008). 'The Enterprising Self: An Unsuitable Job for an Older Worker'. *Organization*, 15(3), 389–405.

Alter, A. (2020). 'Bookstores Are Struggling. Is a New E-Commerce Site the Answer?' *The New York Times*, 16 June.

Alvarez, S. A., and Barney, J. B. (2007). 'Discovery and Creation: Alternative Theories of Entrepreneurial Action'. *Strategic Entrepreneurship Journal*, 1(1–2), 11–26.

Alvarez, S., and Barney, J. B. (2020). 'Has the Concept of Opportunities Been Fruitful In the Field of Entrepreneurship?' *Academy of Management Perspectives*, 34(3), 300–10.

Alvesson, M., and Willmott, H. (2002). 'Identity Regulation as Organizational Control: Producing the Appropriate Individual'. *Journal of Management Studies*, 39(5), 619–44.

Alvesson, M., Lee Ashcraft, K., and Thomas, R. (2008). 'Identity Matters: Reflections on the Construction of Identity Scholarship in Organization Studies'. *Organization*, 15(1), 5–28.

Anderson, A. R., and Warren, L. (2011). 'The Entrepreneur as Hero and Jester: Enacting the Entrepreneurial Discourse'. *International Small Business Journal*, 29(6), 589–609.

Anderson, A. R., Warren, L., and Bensemann, J. (2019). 'Identity, Enactment, and Entrepreneurship Engagement in a Declining Place'. *Journal of Small Business Management*, 57(4), 1559–77.

Audretsch, D. B., Lehmann, E. E., and Seitz, N. (2019). 'Amenities, Subcultures, and Entrepreneurship'. *Small Business Economics*, 9(1), 571–91.

Authors Guild (2020). AG Statement on Proposed Sale of Simon & Schuster and Its Ramifications for Authors, 25 November. www .authorsguild.org/industry-advocacy/ag-statement-on-proposed-sale-of-simon-schuster-and-its-ramifications-for-authors/

Baines, S., and an Wheelock, J. (1998). 'Working for Each Other: Gender, the Household and Micro-Business Survival and Growth'. *International Small Business Journal*, 17(1), 16–35.

Baron, R. A., and Ward, T. B. (2004). 'Expanding Entrepreneurial Cognition's Toolbox: Potential Contributions from the Field of Cognitive Science'. *Entrepreneurship Theory and Practice*, 28(6), 553–73.

Bartel, C. A., and Garud, R. (2009). 'The Role of Narratives in Sustaining Organizational Innovation'. *Organization Science*, 20(1), 107–17.

Baum, J. R., Frese, M., and Baron, R. A. (2014). 'Born to Be an Entrepreneur? Revisiting the Personality Approach to Entrepreneurship'. In Baum, Freese, and Baron (eds.) *The Psychology of Entrepreneurship*. East Sussex: Psychology Press, pp. 73–98.

Baumol, W. J., Litan, R. E., and Schramm, C. J. (2007). *Good Capitalism, Bad Capitalism, and the Economics of Growth and Prosperity*. New Haven, CT: Yale University Press.

Beaucage, A., Laplante, N., and Legare, R. (2004). 'The Shift to Self-Employment: An Imposed Choice or an Obvious Choice?' *Industrial Relations*, 59(2).

Bjursell, C., and Melin, L. (2011). 'Proactive and Reactive Plots: Narratives in Entrepreneurial Identity Construction'. *International Journal of Gender and Entrepreneurship*, 3(3), 218–35.

Block, J., and Koellinger, P. (2009). 'I Can't Get No Satisfaction – Necessity Entrepreneurship and Procedural Utility'. *Kyklos*, 62(2), 191–209.

Bögenhold, D., and Klinglmair, A. (2016). 'Independent Work, Modern Organizations and Entrepreneurial Labor: Diversity and Hybridity of Freelancers and Self-Employment'. *Journal of Management & Organization*, 22(6), 843–58.

Bold, M. R. (2016). 'An "Accidental Profession": Small Press Publishing in the Pacific Northwest'. *Publishing Research Quarterly*, 32(2), 84–102.

Bolton, W. K., and Thompson, J. L. (2000). *Entrepreneurs: Talent, Tempérament, Technique*. Oxford: Butterworth Heinemann.

Boog, J. (2019). 'Publishers Brace for California Labor Law Changes'. *Publishers Weekly*, 17 December. https://www.publishersweekly.com/pw/by-topic/industry-news/publisher-news/article/81992-publishers-brace-for-california-labor-law-changes.html.

Brandstätter, H. (2011). 'Personality Aspects of Entrepreneurship: A Look at Five Meta-Analyses'. *Personality and Individual Differences*, 51(3), 222–30.

Bridges, L. E. (2018). 'Flexible as Freedom? The Dynamics of Creative Industry Work and the Case Study of the Editor in Publishing'. *New Media & Society*, 20(4), 1303–19.

Brown, A. D. (2006). 'A Narrative Approach to Collective Identities'. *Journal of Management Studies*, 43(4), 731–53.

Brown, S. (ed.). (2006). *Consuming Books: The Marketing and Consumption of Literature*. London: Routledge.

Bruni, A., Gherardi, S., and Poggio, B. (2004). *Gender and Entrepreneurship: An Ethnographic Approach*. AbingdonA: Routledge.

Brush, C. G., de Bruin, A., and Welter, F. A. (2009). 'Gender-Aware Framework for Women's Entrepreneurship'. *International Journal of Gender and Entrepreneurship*, 1(1), 8–24.

Bruyat, C., and Julien, P. A. (2001). 'Defining the Field of Research in Entrepreneurship'. *Journal of Business Venturing*, 16(2), 165–80.

Burke, A. (2011). 'The Entrepreneurship Enabling Role of Freelancers: Theory with Evidence from the Construction Industry'. *International Review of Entrepreneurship*, 9(3), 131–58.

Burke, A. E. (2015). *The Handbook of Research on Freelancing and Self-Employment*, Foxrock, Dublin: Senate Hall Academic Publishing.

Burke, A., and Cowling, M. (2020). 'The Role of Freelancers in Entrepreneurship and Small Business'. *Small Business Economics*, 55(2), 389–92.

Burke, A., Zawwar, I., and Hussels, S. (2020). 'Do Freelance Independent Contractors Promote Entrepreneurship?' *Small Business Economics* 55 (2), 415–27.

Burtch, G., Carnahan, S., and Greenwood, B. N. (2018). 'Can You Gig It? An Empirical Examination of the Gig Economy and Entrepreneurial Activity'. *Management Science*, 64(12), 5497–520.

Byrne, O., and Shepherd, D. A. (2015). 'Different Strokes for Different Folks: Entrepreneurial Narratives of Emotion, Cognition, and Making Sense of Business Failure'. *Entrepreneurship Theory and Practice*, 39(2), 375–405.

Carbado, D. W., Crenshaw, K. W., Mays, V. M., and Tomlinson, B. (2013). 'Intersectionality: Mapping the Movements of a Theory'. *Du Bois Review: Social Science Research on Race*, 10(2), 303–12.

Cardon, M. S., Gregoire, D. A., Stevens, C. E., and Patel, P. C. (2013). 'Measuring Entrepreneurial Passion: Conceptual Foundations and Scale Validation'. *Journal of Business Venturing*, 28(3), 373–96.

Carson, D., Cromie, S., McGowan, P., and Hill, J. (1995). *Marketing and Entrepreneurship in SMEs: An Innovative Approach*. New York: Pearson Education.

Casson, M., Yeung, B., Basu, A., and Wadeson, N. (2008). *The Oxford Handbook of Entrepreneurship*. New York: Oxford University Press.

Chell, E., Wicklander, D. E., Sturman, S. G., and Hoover, L. W. (2008). *The Entrepreneurial Personality: A Social Construction*, 2nd ed., London: Routledge.

Chetty, R., Grusky, D., Hell, M., Hendren, N., Manduca, R., and Narang, J. (2016). *The Fading American Dream: Trends in Absolute Income Mobility Since 1940.* National Bureau of Economic Research Working Paper Series. https://opportunityinsights.org/paper/the-fading-american-dream/

Cohen, L., and Musson, G. (2000). 'Entrepreneurial Identities: Reflections from Two Case Studies'. *Organization*, 7(1), 31–48.

Colli, A., Pérez, P. F., and Rose, M. B. (2003). 'National Determinants of Family Firm Development? Family Firms in Britain, Spain, and Italy in the Nineteenth and Twentieth Centuries'. *Enterprise & Society*, 4(1), 28–64.

Courty, P. and Pagliero, M. (2013). 'The Pricing of Art and the Art of Pricing: Pricing Styles in the Concert Industry', in Victor A. Ginsburgh and David Throsby (eds.), *Handbook of the Economics of Art and Culture Vol. 2* (1st ed.). Amsterdam: North Holland, pp. 299–356.

Crenshaw, K. (1989). 'Demarginalizing the Intersection of Race and Sex: A Black Feminist Critique of Antidiscrimination Doctrine, Feminist Theory and Antiracist Politics'. University of Chicago Legal Forum, 139. https://chicagounbound.uchicago.edu/uclf/vol1989/iss1/8.

Cullen, J. (2003). *The American Dream: A Short History of an Idea that Shaped a Nation.* New York: Oxford University Press.

Damian, D., and Capatina, A. (2019). 'Seeking Freelancers' Motivations to Adopt an Entrepreneurial Career: A Storytelling Approach'. *Proceedings of the International Conference on Business Excellence*, 13(1), 206–15.

Das, J. (2007). 'Sydney Freelance Journalists and the Notion of Professionalism'. *Pacific Journalism Review: Te Koakoa*, 13(1), 142–60.

Dempster, A. M. (2009). 'An Operational Risk Framework for the Performing Arts and Creative Industries'. *Creative Industries Journal*, 1 (2), 151–70.

Dentoni, D., Pascucci, S., Poldner, K., and Gartner, W. B. (2018). 'Learning "Who We Are" by Doing: Processes of Co-Constructing Prosocial Identities in Community-Based Enterprises'. *Journal of Business Venturing, Enterprise Before and Beyond Benefit, Part 2: Prosocial Organizing*, 33(5), 603–22.

Dew, N. (2009). 'Serendipity in Entrepreneurship'. *Organization Studies*, 30 (7), 735–53.

Dollinger, M. (2008). *Entrepreneurship*. Lombard, IL: Marsh Publications.

Down, S. (2006). *Narratives of Enterprise: Crafting Entrepreneurial Self-Identity in a Small Firm.*, Cheltenham/Northampton, MA: Edward Elgar Publishing.

Down, S., and Reveley, J. (2004). 'Generational Encounters and the Social Formation of Entrepreneurial Identity: "Young Guns" and "Old Farts"'. *Organization*, 11(2), 233–50.

Down, S., and Warren, L. (2008). 'Constructing Narratives of Enterprise: Clichés and Entrepreneurial Self-identity'. *International Journal of Entrepreneurial Behavior & Research*, 14(1), 4–23.

Downing, S. (2005). 'The Social Construction of Entrepreneurship: Narrative and Dramatic Processes in the Coproduction of Organizations and Identities'. *Entrepreneurship: Theory and Practice*, 29 (2), 185–204.

Duberley, J., and Carrigan, M. (2013). 'The Career Identities of "Mumpreneurs": Women's Experiences of Combining Enterprise and Motherhood'. *International Small Business Journal*, 31(6), 629–51.

Edstrom, M., and Ladendorf, M. (2012). 'Freelance Journalists as a Flexible Workforce in Media Industries'. *Journalism Practice*, 6(5–6), 711–21.

Ekinsmyth, C. (2014). 'Mothers' Business, Work/Life and the Politics of "Mumpreneurship"'. *Gender, Place & Culture*, 21(10), 1230–48.

Equitable Growth (18 February 2020). 'Race and the Lack of Intergenerational Economic Mobility in the United States'. In *Vision*

2020: Evidence for a Stronger Economy. www.equitablegrowth.org/race-and-the-lack-of-intergenerational-economic-mobility-in-the-united-states/

Essers, C., and Benschop, Y. (2007). 'Enterprising Identities: Female Entrepreneurs of Moroccan or Turkish Origin in the Netherlands'. *Organization Studies*, 28(1), 49–69.

Fillis, I. (2006). A Biographical Approach to Researching Entrepreneurship in the Smaller Firm. *Management Decision*, 44(2), 198–212.

Fillis, I. (2015). 'Biographical Research as a Methodology for Understanding Entrepreneurial Marketing'. *International Journal of Entrepreneurial Behavior & Research*, 21(3), 429–47.

Fillis, I., and Rentschler, R. (2010). 'The Role of Creativity in Entrepreneurship'. *Journal of Enterprising Culture*, 18(1), 49–81. https://doi.org/10.1142/S0218495810000501

Florida, R., and Seman, M. (2020). 'Lost Art: Measuring COVID-19's Devastating Impact on America's Creative Economy'. www.brookings.edu/wp-content/uploads/2020/08/20200810_Brookingsmetro_Covid19-and-creative-economy_Final.pdf

Fletcher, D. E. (2006). 'Entrepreneurial Processes and the Social Construction of Opportunity'. *Entrepreneurship & Regional Development*, 18(5), 421–40.

Foss, L. (2004). '"Going Against the Grain ..." Construction of Entrepreneurial Identity Through Narratives', in D. Hjorth and C. Steyaert (eds.), Narrative and Discursive Approaches in Entrepreneurship: A Second Movements in Entrepreneurship Book. Cheltenham: Edward Elgar.

Frey, C. and Keenan, B. (2021). EFA Statement on the PRO Act. Editorial Freelancers Association. www.the-efa.org/efa-statement-on-the-pro-act/#:~:text=The%20Editorial%20Freelancers%20Association%20(EFA,842

Gannon, M. (2016). 'Race Is a Social Construct, Scientists Argue'. *Scientific American*, 5 February.

Gartner, W. B. (2007). 'Entrepreneurial Narrative and a Science of the Imagination'. *Journal of Business Venturing*, 22(5), 613–27.

Garud, R., Gehman, J., and Giuliani, A. P. (2014). 'Contextualizing Entrepreneurial Innovation: A Narrative Perspective'. *Research Policy*, 43(7), 1177–88.

Gehman, J., and Soublière, J. F. (2017). 'Cultural Entrepreneurship: From Making Culture to Cultural Making'. *Innovation*, 19(1), 61–73.

Goktan, A. B., and Gunay, G. (2011). 'Is Entrepreneurial Cognition Culturally Bound? A Comparative Study Conducted in Turkey and the United States'. *Journal of Small Business and Entrepreneurship*, 24 (4), 455–70.

Griswold, W., and Wohl, H. (2015). 'Evangelists of Culture: One Book Programs and the Agents Who Define Literature, Shape Tastes, and Reproduce Regionalism'. *Poetics*, 50, 96–109.

Hamilton, E. (2006). 'Whose Story Is It Anyway? Narrative Accounts of the Role of Women in Founding and Establishing Family Businesses'. *International Small Business Journal*, 24(3), 253–71.

Hamilton, E. (2014). 'Entrepreneurial Narrative Identity and Gender: A Double Epistemological Shift'. *Journal of Small Business Management*, 52(4), 703–12.

Hane, E. and Zats, L. (2020). 'Letter to the Editor: Why These Agents Argue Books Aren't Essential'. *Publishers Weekly*, 28 April.

Hang, M., and Weezel, A. van. (2007). 'Media and Entrepreneurship: What Do We Know and Where Should We Go?' *Journal of Media Business Studies*, 4(1), 51–70.

Henry, C. (2007). *Entrepreneurship in the Creative Industries: An International Perspective*, Cheltenham/Northampton, MA: Edward Elgar Publishing.

Henry, C., Nelson, T., and Lewis, K. (2017). *The Routledge Companion to Global Female Entrepreneurship*. London: Routledge.

Hjorth, D., and Steyaert, C. (2004). 'Narrative and Discursive Approaches in Entrepreneurship: A Second Movements in Entrepreneurship Book'. *University of Illinois at Urbana-Champaign's Academy for Entrepreneurial Leadership Historical Research Reference in Entrepreneurship*.

Hytti, U. (2005). 'New Meanings for Entrepreneurs: from Risk-Taking Heroes to Safe-Seeking Professionals'. *Journal of Organizational Change Management*, 18, 594–611.

Johansson, A. W. (2004). 'Narrating the Entrepreneur'. *International Small Business Journal*, 22(3), 273–93.

Jones, P., Higgins, D., and Trehan, K. (2015). *Celebrating Entrepreneurial and Small Firm Research: Embracing Qualitative Research Philosophies and Methods*. Bingley: Emerald Publishing Limited. http://ebookcentral .proquest.com/lib/psu/detail.action?docID=2070189

Jones, R., Latham, J., and Betta, M. (2008). 'Narrative Construction of the Social Entrepreneurial Identity'. *International Journal of Entrepreneurial Behavior and Research*, 14(5), 330–45.

Kärreman, D., and Alvesson, M. (2004). 'Cages in Tandem: Management Control, Social Identity, and Identification in a Knowledge-Intensive Firm. *Organization*, 11(1), 149–75.

Katz, J. A., and Shepherd, D. A. (2003). *Cognitive Approaches to Entrepreneurship Research*. Vol. VI of *Advances in Entrepreneurship, Firm Emergence and Growth*. Bingley: Emerald Group Publishing Limited.

Kephart, P., and Schumacher, L. (2005). 'Has the "Glass Ceiling" Cracked? An Exploration of Women Entrepreneurship'. *Journal of Leadership & Organizational Studies*, 12(1), 2–15.

Kimura, J. (2019). 'A Cover is Worth 1000 Words: Visibility and Racial Diversity in Young Adult Cover Design'. *PDX Scholar*. https://pdxscholar

.library.pdx.edu/cgi/viewcontent.cgi?article=1035&context=eng_bookpubpaper

Kirsch, J. (2020). 'California's New Labor Law, AB-5, and What It Means for Publishers'. *Independent Book Publishers Association*. 17 January. www.ibpa-online.org/news/485314/Californias-New-Labor-Law-AB-5-and-What-It-Means-for-Publishers.htm

Klamer, A. (2011). 'Cultural Entrepreneurship'. *The Review of Austrian Economics*, 24(2), 141–56. https://doi.org/10.1007/s11138-011-0144-6

Kondo, Dorinne K. (1990). *Crafting Selves: Power, Gender, and Discourses of Identity in a Japanese Workplace*. Chicago: University of Chicago Press.

Konrad, E. D. (2013). 'Cultural Entrepreneurship: The Impact of Social Networking on Success: Cultural Entrepreneurship'. *Creativity and Innovation Management*, 22(3), 307–19.

Koudstaal, M., Sloof, R., and Van Praag, M. (2016). 'Risk, Uncertainty, and Entrepreneurship: Evidence from a Lab-in-the-Field Experiment'. *Management Science*, 62(10), 2897–915.

Larson, G. S., and Pearson, A. R. (2012). 'Placing Identity: Place as a Discursive Resource for Occupational Identity Work Among High-Tech Entrepreneurs'. *Management Communication Quarterly*, 26 (2), 241–66.

Larty, J., and Hamilton, E. (2011). 'Structural Approaches to Narrative Analysis in Entrepreneurship Research: Exemplars from Two Researchers'. *International Small Business Journal*, 29(3), 220–37.

Leeandlowbooks (2020). 'Where Is the Diversity in Publishing? The 2019 Diversity Baseline Survey Results'. 28 January. Lee & Low Books: The Open Book Blog. https://blog.leeandlow.com/2020/01/28/2019diversitybaselinesurvey/

Leitch, C. M., and Harrison, R. T. (2016). 'Identity, Identity Formation and Identity Work in Entrepreneurship: Conceptual Developments and

Empirical Applications'. *Entrepreneurship and Regional Development*, 28 (3–4), 177–90.

Lewis, P. (2010). '"Mumpreneurs": Revealing the Post-feminist Entrepreneur'. In P. Lewis and R. Simpson, eds., *Revealing and Concealing Gender: Issues of Visibility in Organizations*. London: Palgrave Macmillan UK, pp. 124–38.

Lewis, P. (2013). 'The Search for an Authentic Entrepreneurial Identity: Difference and Professionalism among Women Business Owners'. *Gender, Work and Organization*, 20(3), 252–66.

Lounsbury, M., and Glynn, M. A. (2019). *Cultural Entrepreneurship: A New Agenda for the Study of Entrepreneurial Processes and Possibilities*. Cambridge: Cambridge University Press.

Lyons, G. (2019). 'An Indie Alternative to Amazon?' *Poets and Writers*, 12 December. www.pw.org/content/an_indie_alternative_to_amazon

Maher, J. (2020). 'S&S Partners with Bookshop.org'. *Publishers Weekly*, 31 March.

Mathisen, B. R. (2017). 'Entrepreneurs and Idealists: Freelance Journalists at the Intersection of Autonomy and Constraints'. *Journalism Practice*, 11 (7), 909–24.

McAuley, A., and Fillis, I. (2005). 'Careers and Lifestyles of Craft Makers in the 21st Century'. *Cultural Trends*, 14(2), 139–56.

McIlroy, Thad. (2017). 'An Authoritative Look at Book Publishing Startups in the United States'. http://thefutureofpublishing.com/new/wp-content/uploads/2017/01/BookPublishingStartups-McIlroy.pdf

Miller, L. J. (2006). *Reluctant Capitalists: Bookselling and the Culture of Consumption*. Chicago: University of Chicago Press.

Milliot, J. (2020a). 'A Surprisingly Strong Year of Book Sales Continues'. *Publishers Weekly*, 9 October.

Milliot, J. (2020b). 'Bertelsmann to Buy S&S for $2.2 Billion'. *Publishers Weekly*, 25 November.

Milliot, J. (2021). 'Print Book Sales Rose 8.2% in 2020'. *Publishers Weekly*, 7 January.

Mirchandani, K. (1999). 'Feminist Insight on Gendered Work: New Directions in Research on Women and Entrepreneurship'. *Gender, Work & Organization*, 6(4), 224–35.

Morgan, J., Orzen, H., Sefton, M., and Sisak, D. (2016). 'Strategic and Natural Risk in Entrepreneurship: An Experimental Study'. *Journal of Economics & Management Strategy*, 25(2), 420–54.

Morris, M. H., Kuratko, D. F., Schindehutte, M., and Spivack, A. J. (2012). 'Framing the Entrepreneurial Experience'. *Entrepreneurship Theory and Practice*, 36(1), 11–40.

Mulholland, K. (1996). 'Gender Power and Property Relations within Entrepreneurial Wealthy Families'. *Gender, Work & Organization*, 3(2), 78–102.

Murray, S. (2006). 'Publishing Studies: Critically Mapping Research in Search of a Discipline'. *Publishing Research Quarterly*, 22(4), 3–25.

Murray, S. (2018). *The Digital Literary Sphere: Reading, Writing, and Selling Books in the Internet Era*. Baltimore: John Hopkins University Press.

Murray, S. (2020). *Introduction to Contemporary Print Culture: Books as Media*. London: Routledge.

National Assembly of State Arts Agencies (2020). 'Facts and Figures on the Creative Economy'. https://nasaa-arts.org/nasaa_research/facts-figures-on-the-creative-economy/

National Urban League (2020). 'State of Black America: Unmasked'. http://sobadev.iamempowered.com/sites/soba.iamempowered.com/files/NUL-SOBA-2020-ES-web.pdf

Naude, M. J., and Chiweshe, N. (2017). 'A Proposed Operational Risk Management Framework for Small and Medium Enterprises'. *South African Journal of Economic and Management Sciences*, 20(1), 1–10.

Nawotka, E. (2021a). 'Authors Guild Asks Members to Support PRO Act'. *Publishers Weekly*, 1 April.

Nawotka, E. (2021b). 'Bookshop and Libro Post Strong Sales in 2020'. *Publishers Weekly*, 8 January.

Nawotka, E. (2020c). 'Sales Skyrocket at Libro.fm and Bookshop.org'. *Publishers Weekly*, 16 March.

Nicholson, L., and Anderson, A. R. (2005). 'News and Nuances of the Entrepreneurial Myth and Metaphor: Linguistic Games in Entrepreneurial Sense-Making and Sense-Giving'. *Entrepreneurship Theory and Practice*, 29(2), 153–72.

Noorda, R. (2019). 'The Discourse and Value of Being an Independent Publisher'. *Mémoires du livre / Studies in Book Culture*, 10(2).

Ollila, S., Middleton, K., and Donnellon, A. (2012). 'Entrepreneurial Identity Construction: What Does Existing Literature Tell Us?' Institute of Small Business and Entrepreneurship Conference.

Oo, P. P., Allison, T. H., Sahaym, A., and Juasrikul, S. (2019). 'User Entrepreneurs' Multiple Identities and Crowdfunding Performance: Effects through Product Innovativeness, Perceived Passion, and Need Similarity'. *Journal of Business Venturing*, 34(5), 105895.

Osborne, H. (2016). *The Rise of the Modernist Bookshop: Books and the Commerce of Culture in the Twentieth Century*. London: Routledge.

Pagano, A., Petrucci, F., and Bocconcelli, R. (2018). 'A Business Network Perspective on Unconventional Entrepreneurship: A Case from the Cultural Sector'. *Journal of Business Research*, 92, 455–64.

Phillips, N., Tracey, P., and Karra, N. (2013). 'Building Entrepreneurial Tie Portfolios through Strategic Homophily: The Role of Narrative Identity Work in Venture Creation and Early Growth'. *Journal of Business Venturing* Special Issue: Institutions, Entrepreneurs, Community, 28(1), 134–50.

Powell, E. E., and Baker, T. (2014). 'It's What You Make of It: Founder Identity and Enacting Strategic Responses to Adversity'. *Academy of Management Journal*, 57(5), 1406–33.

Reed II, A., Forehand, M. R., Puntoni, S., and Warlop, L. (2012). 'Identity-Based Consumer Behavior'. *International Journal of Research in Marketing*, 29(4), 310–21.

Reid, E. (2015). 'Embracing, Passing, Revealing, and the Ideal Worker Image: How People Navigate Expected and Experienced Professional Identities'. *Organization Science*, 26(4), 997–1017.

Rigg, C., and O'Dwyer, B. (2012). 'Becoming an Entrepreneur: Researching the Role of Mentors in Identity Construction'. *Education + Training*, 54(4), 319–29.

Salamon, E. (2020). 'Digitizing Freelance Media Labor: A Class of Workers Negotiates Entrepreneurialism and Activism'. *New Media and Society*, 22 (1), 105–22.

Samuel, L. R (2012). *The American Dream: A Cultural History*. Syracuse: Syracuse University Press.

Sanchez-Hucles, J. V., and Davis, D. D. (2010). 'Women and Women of Color in Leadership: Complexity, Identity, and Intersectionality'. *American Psychologist*, 65(3), 171–81.

Scott, M. (2012). 'Cultural Entrepreneurs, Cultural Entrepreneurship: Music Producers Mobilising and Converting Bourdieu's Alternative Capitals'. *Poetics*, 40(3), 237–55.

Shane, S. A. (2003). *A General Theory of Entrepreneurship: The Individual-Opportunity Nexus*, Cheltenham/Northampton, MA: Edward Elgar Publishing.

Shane, S., and Venkataraman, S. (2000). 'The Promise of Entrepreneurship as a Field of Research'. *Academy of Management Review*, 25(1), 217–26.

Sikalieh, D., Mokaya, S. O., and Namusonge, M. (2012). 'The Concept of Entrepreneurship; In Pursuit of a Universally Acceptable Definition'.

International Journal of Arts and Commerce, 1(6), 128–35. https://doi.org/10.1016/S2212-23456(14)00039-2.

Smallbone, D., and Kitching, J. (2012). 'Are Freelancers a Neglected Form of Small Business?' *Journal of Small Business and Enterprise Development*, 19(1), 74–91.

Spross, J. (2015). 'Why Workaholics Are Faking Longer Hours – and What That Says about American Businesses'. *The Week*, 14 May. https://theweek.com/articles/554946/why-workaholics-are-faking-longer-hours–what-that-says-about-american-businesses

Squires, C. (2020). 'The Passion and Pragmatism of the Small Publisher'. In G. Colby, K. Marczewska, and L. Wilson (eds.), *The Contemporary Small Press: Making Publishing Visible*, Basingstoke: Palgrave Macmillan, pp. 199–218.

Squires, C. and Murray, P. R. (2013). 'The Digital Publishing Communications Circuit'. *Book 2.0*, 3(1), 3–23.

Stanworth, C., and Stanworth, J. (1997). 'Reluctant Entrepreneurs and Their Clients: The Case of Self-Employed Freelance Workers in the British Book Publishing Industry'. *International Small Business Journal*, 16(1), 58–73.

Statement on Legislation Affecting Freelancers. Editorial Freelancers Association. www.the-efa.org/statement-on-legislation-affecting-freelancers/

Storey, J., Salaman, G., and Platman, K. (2005). 'Living with Enterprise in an Enterprise Economy: Freelance and Contract Workers in the Media'. *Human Relations*, 58(8), 1033–54.

Tajfel, H. (1982). 'Social Psychology of Intergroup Relations'. *Annual Review of Psychology*, 33(1), 1–39.

Thompson, D. (2019). Workism Is Making Americans Miserable. *The Atlantic*, 24 February.

Thompson, J. B. (2012). *Merchants of Culture: The Publishing Business in the Twenty-First Century (2nd ed.)*. Boston: Polity Press.

Towse, R. (2011). *A Handbook of Cultural Economics*. Cheltenham/ Northampton, MA: Edward Elgar Publishing.

US Census Bureau (2012). Survey of Business Owners (SBO): Survey Results: 2012. www.census.gov/library/publications/2012/econ/2012-sbo.html

US Small Business Administration Office of Advocacy (2020). 2020 Small Business Profile. https://cdn.advocacy.sba.gov/wp-content/uploads/2020/06/04144224/2020-Small-Business-Economic-Profile-US.pdf

Valdez, Z. (2011). *The New Entrepreneurs: How Race, Class, and Gender Shape American Enterprise*. Stanford: Stanford University Press.

Vries, N. de, Liebregts, W., and Stel, A. van. (2020). 'Explaining Entrepreneurial Performance of Solo Self-Employed from a Motivational Perspective. *Small Business Economics*, 55(2), 447–60.

Walker, E. (2003). 'Home-Based Businesses: Setting Straight the Urban Myths'. *Small Enterprise Research*, 11(2), 35–48.

Warner, J. (2020). 'Bookshop.org Hopes to Play Rebel Alliance to Amazon's Empire'. *Chicago Tribune*, 15 January.

Warren, L. (2004). 'Negotiating Entrepreneurial Identity: Communities of Practice and Changing Discourses'. *The International Journal of Entrepreneurship and Innovation*, 5(1), 25–35.

Watson, T. J. (2009). 'Entrepreneurial Action, Identity Work and the Use of Multiple Discursive Resources: The Case of a Rapidly Changing Family Business'. *International Small Business Journal*, 27(3), 251–74.

Wiklund, J., Nikolaev, B., Shir, N., Foo, M. D., and Bradley, S. (2019). 'Entrepreneurship and Well-Being: Past, Present, and Future'. *Journal of Business Venturing*, 34(4), 579–88.

Wilding, M. (2018). 'The United States of Workaholics'. *Medium*, 15 March. https://medium.com/s/story/the-united-states-of-workaholics-26ac8a40ae26

Zhao, E. Y., Ishihara, M., and Lounsbury, M. (2013). 'Overcoming the Illegitimacy Discount: Cultural Entrepreneurship in the US Feature Film Industry'. *Organization Studies*, 34(12), 1747–76. https://doi.org/10.1177/0170840613485844

Zhao, H., and Seibert, S. E. (2006). 'The Big Five Personality Dimensions and Entrepreneurial Status: A Meta-analytical Review'. *Journal of Applied Psychology*, 91(2), 259.

Cambridge Elements ≡

Publishing and Book Culture

SERIES EDITOR
Samantha Rayner
University College London

Samantha Rayner is a Reader in UCL's Department of Information Studies. She is also Director of UCL's Centre for Publishing, co-Director of the Bloomsbury CHAPTER (Communication History, Authorship, Publishing, Textual Editing and Reading) and co-editor of the Academic Book of the Future BOOC (Book as Open Online Content) with UCL Press.

ASSOCIATE EDITOR
Leah Tether
University of Bristol

Leah Tether is Professor of Medieval Literature and Publishing at the University of Bristol. With an academic background in medieval French and English literature and a professional background in trade publishing, Leah has combined her expertise and developed an international research profile in book and publishing history from manuscript to digital.

About the Series

This series aims to fill the demand for easily accessible, quality texts available for teaching and research in the diverse and dynamic fields of Publishing and Book Culture. Rigorously researched and peer-reviewed Elements will be published under themes, or 'Gatherings'. These Elements should be the first check point for researchers or students working on that area of publishing and book trade history and practice: we hope that, situated so logically at Cambridge University Press, where academic publishing in the UK began, it will develop to create an unrivalled space where these histories and practices can be investigated and preserved.

A full series listing is available at: www.cambridge.org/EPBC

Printed in the United States
by Baker & Taylor Publisher Services